POLAND

POLAND

INTRODUCTION ■ JACEK ŻAKOWSKI

TEXT ■ IRENA I JERZY KOSTROWICCY

PHOTOGRAPHS ■ MIROSŁAW I MACIEJ CIUNOWICZOWIE

ARKADY

TABLE OF CONTENTS

Introduction

Phoenix on the Plain

For a person such as I – born in Warsaw and one who has spent his whole life in the Polish capital – Poland appears to be one of the most mysterious and exotic places in the world. One may travel across deserts and oceans, the Andes and the prairies of America, Amazonian jungles and the metropolises of the west, and still be astonished by this surprising country which sometimes was also a state, although in the past this was by no means the rule.

We encounter the first mystery while posing an apparently banal question concerning the location of Poland. As we all know, Ubu Roi maintained that the answer is: nowhere. For years, the famous sentence: "In Poland, in other words, nowhere" infuriated the Poles, but it is not as nonsensical as it appears to us. In comparison to other large European countries, the situation of Poland was in this particular respect far from clear.

The wandering country

While studying the political map of Europe from the last centuries we may follow the transference of state borders. Certain states, such as Bohemia, Ukraine, Hungary and the Baltic or Balkan countries, emerged or disappeared. Others, such as Germany, Austria or Prussia, lost and regained parts of their territory on a more or less permanent basis. Only Poland forfeited and gained, appeared and vanished, until finally, more than half a century ago, it traversed several hundred kilometers from the east to the west due to the political decisions made after the second world war by the victorious powers.

History is full of innumerable wandering nations. The same holds true for itinerant states. There was no such thing, however, as a wandering country. Poland is the first country to have accomplished this feat. After all, her transference from the east to the west meant that not only state frontiers and state institutions, i. e. offices and garrisons, shifted, and not only society, in other words, millions of persons were on the move, but that the whole country – entire villages, towns, universities and clinics – was affected. The University of Lwów was revived in Wrocław, and the University of Wilno – in Toruń.

on the right:

Tatra Mts. View of Lake Morskie Oko.

The country which in 1945 wandered from the east to the west, was incomplete, the prime reason being the absence of several millions people, either killed during the war or scattered throughout the world. The second reason lay in the fact that the terrains of the Second Republic left behind by the Poles were full of historical treasures of the Polish heritage: towns and castles, palaces and manors, art collections and even libraries. Just as important as the products of human culture were the former eastern borderlands – Lithuania, the homeland of Polish literature from Mickiewicz to Miłosz, the multinational and multi-religious western Ukraine, the forests and marshes of Belorussia, inhabited by romantic spirits, forefathers' ghosts and the local population.

In place of these spatial, geographic, ethnic, religious, historical and cultural riches, frequently backward but an imminent part of Polishness, Poland was granted the depopulated lands of former eastern Germany. Alien space, an alien landscape and the alien architecture of a partially urbanised and civilised terrain, where the forests of the east had been centuries ago supplanted by cultivated woodlands, the steppes – by tilled fields, thatched-roof cottages – by brick or half-timbered buildings, and sandy or muddy roads – by basalt sett.

Up to this very day I find that in this Germanic landscape the soft, singsong speech and refined culture of Poles from the east produce a cacophonous impression, even stronger considering that, paradoxically, the Poles installed in this alien landscape had been for the first time in their history sentenced to live among themselves. After all, Poland has never been a strictly national state. Polish towns were always multinational, multicultural, multi-religious and multi-linguistic. The Jews, the Germans and the Ukrainians created them to a degree equal to that of the Poles. In the small towns of central and eastern Poland Yiddish was often a language more popular than Polish. The countryside in the east was to a great extent Ruthenian, Ukrainian, Belorussian and Lithuanian. The Polish pre-war Parliament was a miniature United Nations, in which the Poles sat side by side with the Jews, the Ukrainians, the Lithuanians, the Belorussians and the Germans. Here, the Polish language was a *sui generis* Latin – a common language which for some of the deputies remained a foreign tongue. For Polishness and Poland which, as Tomasz Jastrun wrote, lies "on the crossroads of Asia and Europe", the multicultural phenomenon was of essential, constitutive significance and acted as a prominent motor force.

The syncretic quality – from the apparel of the gentry to religiosity and architecture – was a constant element of Polish identity. It is difficult to disregard it while examining photographs of the most sacred sites. The face of the Madonna of Jasna Góra reflects Byzantium. The architecture of Wawel Castle or the Cracow Cloth Halls echoes Italian Renaissance. This trait become even more noticeable while studying the affiliations of the greatest names in Polish culture. Our national poem begins with the words: "Lithuania, my homeland..." and the *Dąbrowski Mazurka* is performed in it by a Jewish cymbalist. Not by accident did Fryderyk Chopin, the author of the quintessence of Polish music, have a foreign sounding surname. Polish twentieth -century poetry was to a large extent written by authors of Jewish descent. A great role in Polish science and the humanities was played by professors with German and Jewish names – Kolberg, Natanson, Hoyer, Bruckner, Estreicher and Zoll. After the second world war Poland was brutally deprived of a great part of the sources of this inspiration, and for the first time in her history she became, for all practical purposes, a single-nation country.

Sulmierzyce. Wooden town hall with arcades from 1743, today: Regional Museum.

on the left:
Milicz.
Church of St. Andrzej Bobola from 1709, formerly Protestant.

The archaeology of discontinuity

The painful stumps displayed by contemporary Polishness are the remnants not only of ethnic minorities and vanished land. The second world war and communism, brutally introduced after the war, ruthlessly cut across the Polish social fibre. During the 1940s the higher social strata, created throughout the past centuries, were politically, economically, socially and, to a large degree, biologically destroyed. A large part was intentionally annihilated by the German and Soviet occupants, some perished in the underground struggle waged against fascism and communism, and others opted for emigration.

The rest, deprived of property and social rank, was regarded by the communists as a "class enemy" and, as a rule, barely survived on the margin of official life. By resorting to an organic metaphor one might say that a country which had lost a large fragment of its roots and multi-ethnic limbs was additionally deprived of a large section of its head. This was not all. At the same time, the rest of Polish society was subjected to a social experiment.

Wincenty
Kasprzycki,
*View of Natolin
Palace from the
Courtyard.*

The parceling of land, the campaign against the "kulaks" (prosperous peasants) and collectivization in the countryside shattered the traditional structures of the peasant communities and affected the landscape from which signs of the previous order of things disappeared unexpectedly rapidly. When as a teenager I traveled across Poland, partially on foot and partly as a hitchhiker, I frequently came across strangely picturesque, tree-lined avenues which unexpectedly came to an abrupt end several hundred meters from the village buildings on sites where mysteriously scattered old trees, stones, fragments of a wall

or underpinning, columns or simply mounds concealing unexplored historical traces would appear among amidst fields or groves. I was fond of such places and especially of imagining how they must have looked decades earlier: the location of a manor house, a porch, a bower, a path leading to a pond, a flower bed and a driveway encircling it. Upon certain occasions all could be recreated rather easily. At other times, it became necessary to infer from the arrangement of the trees, pits and unkempt rose bushes, since the traces of a small manor house, dismantled to the last brick, could be easily mistaken for those of a large bower or a stable.

Not only the studies of the countryside call for the skills of an archaeologist. In contrast to the majority of European countries Poland is full of abandoned, haphazardly refashioned and carelessly transposed sites. In addition, there are places which despite wars and years of communism have preserved their original appearance – every small and larger town and every more prominent object conceal mysteries and inspire speculation, exercise our imagination, and encourage to recreate former functions, orders and meanings. Was this cinema once a synagogue? Or perhaps its building contained the riding school of a tsarist garrison?

Was this school once a monastery? And if so, then of what order? When did its cassation take place? What succeeded the monastery? Barracks? A prison? A hospital? What is this building? The residence of a governor? A stable? A palace of the local bishop or magnate, without the original colonnade? What did the present-day cultural centre house in the past? What about the library, the office of the starosta, the municipal offices...? Is it true that the playing ground behind the cinema was once a cemetery which the communist authorities ordered to level? What was the religion of the deceased?

Aleksander Rafałowski,
*Landscape
from Bodzentyn.*

Whose bones are being washed out by the rain on the overgrown hillock next to the wood? Catholics? The Russian Orthodox? Jews? Protestants? Or perhaps Moslems? In this sense, Poland remains a great puzzle. Today not much seems to be in its own place or to fulfil a suitable function. Even the Old Town in Warsaw, destroyed by the Germans and rebuilt after the war – at first glance, meticulously recreated in its smallest details – does not really constitute a 500-years old fragment of the capital. After all, it was not repopulated by prewar residents, nor does it contain prewar shops and thus is devoid of the climate, ambience and character of bygone days. Even Cracow – the best preserved large Polish city – displays a gaping wound in the district of Kazimierz, the former Jewish quarter, and a troublesome growth in the shape of Nowa Huta, a conception devised by planners and a glaring foreign body within the municipal structure and landscape. Łódź without its German, Russian and Jewish inhabitants and plutocracy, whose only traces are the rather absurd palatial residences, still cannot regain its identity.

What about Warsaw, completely ravaged during the second world war? Partially rebuilt and partly supplemented according to consecutive needs, tastes, trends and opportunities, it remains at almost every step of the way amazingly inconsistent and displays multi-hued additions.

It seems worth keeping all those facts in mind while glancing through the magnificent photographs of Poland. Whenever a photograph shows something else than nature, then despite the mastery of the artist we frequently notice a certain gap, as if the depicted world has not been fully revived. The photographs appear to disclose a certain deficit of vitality, as if some sort of a register had not been made or the artist had removed a component. This is not, however, a question of recording nor the fault of the equipment or even more so of the artist. Such a void simply exists in nature, and cannot be captured and named; it seems much easier to identify it by comparing the album about Poland with similar publications about countries which experienced history quite differently. It then becomes

Radziejowice. Manor house built of larch.

obvious that elsewhere the strings of historical bonds that remain so silent in the Polish landscape, resound with a continuum which Poland lacks. In Paris, Rome, Prague, Budapest or even New York the streets, the squares and the houses reverberate with life, assorted roles, customs and functions which assumed shape and grew throughout centuries. Poland also pulsates with life, at times even more intense than in New York or Prague, but as a rule – and this something which we both feel and see – it has been doing so for a much shorter period of time.

While examining these beautiful, albeit at first glance conventional photographs of splendid landscapes, valuable buildings and picturesque streets, we come across traces of the fundamental grief of contemporary Polishness and Poland – distress caused by a lack of continuity. It can be experienced even more strongly while comparing these photographs with those of prewar Poland, which may appear poorer, frequently uglier, more dishevelled and sometimes outright backward in a highly disagreeable or simply shocking way, but strongly enrooted in history, breathing the air of a still alive, centuries-old history, clothed with the dust of bygone ages.

It is precisely this lack of continuity which renders Poland and the Poles, situated in the geographical centre of Europe, so non-European and, at the same time, amazingly similar to America and the Americans. In contrast to the Europeans – the Poles and the Americans are predominantly emigrants or migrants of the first, second or third generation, living in landscapes not quite domesticated, and still seeking a place for themselves.

Against the background of sophisticated Europe we are, in the words of Zbigniew Herbert, "barbarians in a garden". Perhaps this is the reason why sometimes we find it surprisingly difficult to understand our European brothers in Paris or Vienna, and so easily come to terms with other barbarians residing in Detroit, Dallas or Phoenix.

A kaleidoscope of enclaves

A wandering country which suffers from discontinuity is probably a unique phenomenon on a global scale. But this is by no means the end of our list of Polish surprises. Despite all odds, Poland remains, especially from the vantage point of a resident of Warsaw, a great kaleidoscope of lands, landscapes and worlds. An impressive diversity in a country that is sizable but not extensive. In this sense, Poland resembles a botanical garden or a natural history museum with innumerable forms of life amassed in a limited space. It is difficult to share this impression by merely glancing at a spiritless map or even reading descriptions in guidebooks. This diversity be grasped slightly more easily by poring over an album, although here too we encounter barriers of the scale. After all, photographs do not show the distances separating successive objects.

If one wishes to savour this diversity as fully as possible it would be best to take a one-day car trip from Zakopane in the Tatra Mts. to Sopot on the Baltic coast. In not quite ten hours of a leisurely drive our route will lead us from the rocky Tatras *via* the Podhale highlands, the hilly regions of Kraków, industrial Silesia, the extremely picturesque limestone

Ciechocinek.
Spa house.

Świętokrzyskie Mts., a fragment of the sandy desert near Błędów, the plains of Mazovia, the lake district of Mazuria, the Żuławy depression and the moraines of Pomerania to the Baltic beaches. All this in the course of a single day. The attractiveness of this archetypical Polish itinerary, which is worth devoting much more time than a single car journey, lies not only in the landscape. Quite frequently, this picturesque trail offers the most important enclaves of Polish continuity, astonishing and fascinating not only due to the contrast with the rest of the country, but also to the force of their enrootment. If any sort of a continuity has managed to survive all the tides of experiments and turmoil which had swept across Poland, then it must contain a powerful force, easily discernible in the local highlander, Silesian and Kaszubian communities, firmly embedded in history. People who are totally immersed in the same locality for generations, who have never moved or basically changed their lifestyle, who had not experienced war or postwar social experiments, look

Gdynia Orłowo.
Beach.

different and have a different attitude towards the landscape in which they live. The signs of continuity which surround them and which they cultivate with great effectiveness – the traditional shawls or trousers worn daily by the highlanders, the Silesian colourful window frames or aprons, shrines or even the habit of sitting on the threshold, as well as the blue-tinted cottages of Little Poland are the reason why a visitor arriving from the zone of discontinuity senses a strange feeling. I remember this curious longing experienced for the first time when as a secondary school pupil I roamed across Silesia and encountered traditional miners' housing estates in which time had seemed to stop long before the miners' wives had heard that their husbands constitute the avantgarde of progress. I also recall this yearning from my trips in the Podhale region, where successive attempts at modernisation blended with tradition but did not destroy it. Finally, I recollect this impression from my excursions to Mazuria or the Kaszuby region. Quite possibly, by taking a closer look at such enclaves of continuity one may try to imagine what this album would have looked like had history treated Poland differently. One could try to envisage not only Warsaw with the Nalewki district inhabited by the Orthodox Jews, but also Leżajsk full of Chassidic Jews or Łódź with its crowded Piotrowska Street resembling New York's Fifth Avenue, Oxford Street or Unter den Linden. One could also imagine the Old Town in Warsaw with laundry drying in the streets. The same holds true for villages with inhabited manor houses in place of the post-collective farm housing estates, and open taverns, for centuries managed by the same families, instead of co-operative bars. The country inns would probably serve coca-cola instead of lemonade, and cheap whisky next to vodka. A jeep, and not a horse carriage, would probably stand in front of the manor house. The windmill would probably be out of order, and the old water mill would be closed. Nonetheless, something would be no longer missing in the photographs – even if it were to consist of multiple layers of flaking paint documenting the changing tastes of several epochs, a fragment of an old-fashioned inscription visible underneath a modern shop sign, or great grandfather's old carriage, slowly moulding in the shed. That something could also include an expression of self-assurance in the faces of the people who accidentally found themselves in the photograph. Such self-assurance requires more than a roof over one's head or a solid meal; it comes from living for generations in the only secure place on Earth, a place we can call our own.

The year 1989 marked the end of an epoch of twentieth-century European wars and ideological experiments. The Polish Phoenix, which for centuries has lived on the ill-fated plain, is slowly recovering. We have witnessed the return of relatively normal life, the sort in which everyone tries to control his own world in a fashion which he finds convenient and which has not been devised by someone else. The postwar void has began to spontaneously fill in. Naturally, the old world is not coming back, and shall never do so. The lost continuum of time and space cannot be regained. It is, however, possible to retrieve vitality and to domesticate space, a task slowly pursued. Once again, we are taming our small worlds. The route from the Tatra Mts. to the Baltic has become overgrown with hundreds of motels, bars and advertisements of firms whose existence no one even suspected more than a decade ago. Sometime later, those who survive will cherish a tradition of their own and a legend of the first owners; a portrait of the founder will be displayed over the counter. At nighttime, our city centres are no longer moribund. The wartime gaps are being slowly filled with modern supplements, and will gradually become covered with dust and layers of differently coloured paint as well as our heaped belongings; they will display our imprints and become marked with the traces of dreams, both achieved and unfulfilled. Our world too will become domesticated in no more than two generations. This is good news for today's twenty-year olds, who shall probably see a Polish landscape devoid of the scars of discontinuity. Then, it will become necessary to exchange some of the photographs in this album since not only the landscape but the very faces of the Poles will change: they shall feature the certainty that Ubu Roi was wrong; the immediate and unwavering response to the question: "In Poland, in other words, where ?" will be: "Here !".

Jacek Żakowski
For M.C.

The Carpathian Mts. and The Sub-Carpathian Region

A panoramic view of the Tatra Mts. demonstrates the variety of rock shapes and forms, the steep slopes and craggy peaks rising majestically over picturesque valleys. The highest, most precipitous and rugged parts are the mainly granite Eastern Tatra Mts., also known as the High Tatra Mts., with their magnificent dales and mountain meadows, towering summits and mighty mountain massifs. Piles of scree lie at the foot of the perpendicular or almost vertical rock faces, and the gullies are full of broken rock material. The main Tatra ridge contains the Rysy group of peaks. The Slovak-Polish frontier, which runs along this ridge, deflects sharply to the north towards the Podhale region. The highest of the three Rysy mountaintops (2 503 m) is on the Slovak side of the frontier, and the next one (2 499 m) lies along the boundary line. The view from this summit, the highest in the Polish Tatra, is considered to be the most beautiful in the Tatra Mts. On a fine day one can see all the most important pinnacles and mountain ridges, the valleys and lakes, and the basins surrounding the Tatra Mts.

The largest and most beautiful mountain lake in Poland (an area of 34,5 ha) is Morskie Oko (Eye of the Sea), at an altitude of 1 393 m. Its name is derived from old legends about an underground link with the sea. The highlanders also call it "Fish Lake" because its crystal clear waters are the habitat of trout and grayling. Dwarf mountain pines grow on the lake shores; higher still are clumps of spruce, rowan trees and magnificent mountain stone pines. The circular Czarny Staw (Black Lake), the second biggest lake in the Tatra with area of 20.5 ha, is 191 m higher up, in the rocky basin of the Rybi Potok (Fish Stream) Valley. The stream which flows from it runs into Morskie Oko in a series of cascades and small waterfalls.

on the right:

Tatra Mts. View of Roztoka Valley.

From the beginning of the 19th century, the two lakes have been the main tourist attraction of the Tatra Mts. (I. J. K.)

Strążyska Valley, formed by the Strążyski stream with its numerous cascades and the Siklawica Waterfall, is one of the most breathtaking valleys in the Western Tatra Mts. A marked trail to Mt. Giewont (1 909 m) leads through the picturesque groups of rocks and abundant mixed forest. The rock face of Mt. Giewont rises 600 m above the upper parts of the valley. A deep cleft in the ridge of Mt. Giewont endows it with the shape of a profile of a recumbent man, which has given rise to a legend about a sleeping knight. Chochołowska Valley is the westernmost valley in the Polish Tatra Mts. and one of the largest and longest. It has numerous smaller branches, and two sharp contractions form rocky gateways. In the past, iron ore was excavated in the valley. The higher Chochołowska Glade is the site of a large tourist hostel and shepherds' huts, vestiges of the once extensive sheep and cattle grazing. The glade is famous for crocuses blooming in the spring. In the winter, Chochołowska Valley is an attractive skiing area. (I. J. K.)

Within the Carpathian Mts. the Tatra Mts. form a distinct natural habitat for high-mountain flora found in similar climatic conditions in other mountain chains or the far north, including Arctic as well as Central European and Eurasian mountain species. Relic species date from past geological epochs – the Tertiary and Older Quarternary periods. The Tatra flora varies in accordance with the altitude. On the lower level (950-1 250 m above sea level) spruce trees predominate, with groves of grey alder growing along streams and brooks. A dark, spruce forest prevails from 1 250 to 1 550 m. The upper border of the forest contains stone pine and European larch, both rare in Poland. The dwarf mountain pines, dominant between 1 550 and 1 800 m, comprise a dense scrub at lower levels and further up grow in clumps and patches. This is also the furthest range of trees. Strong winds, extreme oscillations of temperature, and a short growing season restrict the

flora to groundling vegetation adapted to the harsh climate. Plant life at the alp level (1 800-2 300 m) consists of characteristic species growing close to the ground, distinct from their lowland counterparts; their differentiation depends predominantly on the type of subsoil. The highest stratum is composed of rocky peaks and crags (above 2 300 m), the only of its sort in Poland. The sparse vegetation consists exclusively of high-mountain plants, whose majority is protected as rare species.

The most known and popular plants, universally regarded the symbols of the Tatra Mts., include the Alpine edelweiss and the carline, although the latter is also found as far away as the Polish Uplands. Both plants are favourite motifs in local folk art. (I. J. K.)

The Tatra fauna is characterised by Alpine species,

especially the chamois and the marmot, which have been under protection since 1868. Rare bears, lynxes and ermines are accompanied by the more common stags and roe deer, badgers, polecats, weasels, martens and, in some parts, wild boars. The Tatra range offers an opportunity to see the magnificent golden eagle; other typical species are the wallcreepers, sparrow hawks, mountain wagtails, water pipets and water ouzels. The spotted salamander, particularly noteworthy for its exquisite colouring, remains distinct among the local amphibians.

Mt. Kasprowy (1 985 m), a border peak in the Western Tatra Mts., rises above a series of beautiful valleys: Goryczkowa, Kasprowa, Gąsienicowa and Cicha, offering a panoramic view of the surrounding peaks and valleys comprising the High and Western Tatra ranges. An astronomical observatory in the vicinity

Tatra Mts.
Lake Morskie Oko
and Mt. Rysy.

on the left:

Tatra Mts.
Strążyska Valley.

of the summit is the highest in Poland. During winter months, the area of Mt. Kasprowy is crossed by excellent ski runs with chair-lifts. As the heart of numerous tourist trails and the source of wonderful vistas, the peak is a popular tourist attraction, reached by a cable car line opened in 1934 and starting in the Kuźnice station in Zakopane. Cable cars pass above Bystra Valley forests to an interchange at the Myślenickie Turnie peak; from here, they reach the Kasprowy terminus. Tourism in the Tatra Mts. boasts a long tradition: hiking, mountain climbing and skiing date back to the 19th century. The eminent Polish scientist Stanisław Staszic, who conducted research in the Tatra Mts. between 1803 and 1805 and scaled, i. a. Mt. Łomnica and Mt. Krywań, is regarded as the precursor of Tatra mountain climbing. The 19th-century tourists were frequently accompanied by highlanders, the residents of Zakopane, who subsequently assumed the role of professional guides. Today, their successors constitute the majority of the members of the Tatra Voluntary Rescue Service, entrusted with the safety of the tourists. During the Nazi occupation, the Tatra guides fulfilled the dangerous function of Resistance couriers. (I. J. K.)

Zakopane, the largest Polish tourist and winter-sports centre and the so-called winter capital of Poland, is situated in a basin known as the Sub-Tatra Rift, at the foot of the northern slopes of the Tatra Mts. between Mt. Giewont and Mt. Gubałówka. This the starting point of numerous tourist trails and ski lifts, as well as a cable car link to Mt. Gubałówka. A ski jump complex on the slopes of Mt. Krokiew is suitable for competitions, including international events. Hot springs in Jaszczurówka and on the

Tatra Mts.
Chochołowska Valley.

on the left:

Tatra Mts.
View from Mt.
Kasprowy.

Zakopane. The "Pod Jedlami" villa built in 1896-1897, designed by Stanisław Witkiewicz.

Antałówka slopes, are the reason why Zakopane developed as a health resort. The town, situated at an altitude of 800-1 000 m, evolved from a 16th-century village. During the 17th century, a mining-iron foundry centre operated in Kuźnice, the highest part of Zakopane, and was still functioning in the 19th century. By this time, the town was becoming a tourist centre. The first recorded mountaineering expeditions date back to the late 18th century, and the first hostel was built in 1823. The actual devel-opment of Zakopane began in earnest during the 19th century. In about 1870, Dr. Tytus Chałubiński, the co-founder of the Tatra Society, established in 1873, popularised the climatic-therapeutic merits and beauty of the Tatra mountains. The number of visitors, holidaymakers and people seeking to repair their health increased. The tourist trade expanded, especially once the town was connected by rail with the rest of the country (1899). Zakopane became a favourite destination of the intellectual and artistic elites of Cracow (Kraków) and Warsaw (Warszawa), and after the regaining of independence, of visitors from all over Poland. Municipal status was granted in 1933. During the second world war, Zakopane, closed to Polish tourists, assumed the rank of a resort intended for the Nazi military and dignitaries. At the same time, it became a conveyance centre for the Polish Resistance movement. Today, the number of tourists, vastly exceeding that of permanent residents, is estimated at several million people annually, whose major part stays in Zakopane itself. Krupówki Street, the main thoroughfare, concentrating social life and commerce, is closed to traffic and has become as busy as a metropolitan promenade. Zakopane is the site of assorted sports events and artistic meetings, some of which are connected with local folklore and the vibrant tradition of the Podhale highlanders. (I. J. K.)

The development of Zakopane entailed changes in the building style. The old timber houses and farmsteads of the highlanders, made of thick beams and covered with steep shingle roofs, were supplemented by villas whose forms referred to the traditional style, for instance, the "Pod Jedlami" villa designed by Stanisław Witkiewicz, the author of the so-called Zakopane style. Modern buildings, especially those constructed during the 1960s and 1970s, abandoned the old style. In its capacity as a prominent health and tourist resort Zakopane has many sanatoria, tourist facilities, pensionnats and hotels, alongside preserved examples of original highland architecture and art. Valuable ethnographic and geological collections as well as examples of Tatra flora and fauna are featured in the Tatra Museum, founded in 1888. In 1972, the Karol Szymanowski Museum was opened in the "Atma" villa, where the composer lived and worked: here he composed *Harnasie*, a ballet based on highland motifs. (I. J. K.)

For centuries, itinerant shepherds (Polish: *juhas*) have used the high meadows (*hale*) for seasonal grazing. In the spring, they drove the flocks of sheep belonging to whole villages into the mountains under the supervision of a head shepherd known as *baca*. Upon arrival, they moved into wooden huts, and were helped by white sheepdogs of the Podhale breed. In their shelters, the shepherds would process ewes' milk into assorted varieties of cheese called *bunc*, *bryndza*, *oscypek*. Shepherding

Zakopane. Chapel in Jaszczurówka from 1908, designed by Stanisław Witkiewicz.

was associated with unique customs, and special utensils were used for storing and processing the milk. Itinerant sheep grazing, formerly the occupation of the highlanders inhabiting the extensive Podhale basin, has been supplanted by farming. Pastures have been greatly reduced once grazing was prohibited in the Tatra National Park. The spring and autumn *redyk* , i. e. the driving of the sheep to the mountain pastures and bringing them back down before the onset of cold weather, still takes place, although in a changed form. Today, the sheep are taken by train to the Low Beskid, Bieszczady and Sudety Mts.

The villages of the Podhale region have retained their rich, viable and picturesque highland folklore. The region was settled in the Middle Ages by inhabitants of the Cracow area, German colonists and Wallachian shepherds. It was also affected by the impact of Hungarian, Slovakian and Gypsy culture. The specific folklore, fascinating and varied, produced by this ethnic mixture, is reflected up to this day in the costumes, worn especially on religious holidays and during assorted festivities. Men use trousers of thick white, woollen cloth embroidered with a characteristic motif (*parzenica*), embroidered sleeveless sheepskin waistcoats (*serdak*), and stiff round hats with a crown decorated with small shells. Wide leather belts and moccasins (*kierpce*) made of embossed leather complete the costume. Younger women dress in laced bodices embroidered with floral motifs inspired by the local plants, worn over richly embellished linen blouses; flowery skirts whirl in the local dances whose characteristic feature, especially the dance of the brigands (*zbójnicki*), is their spectacular tempo. (I. J. K)

The Podhale region has managed to maintain its traditional folk arts and crafts. Wood was used for building both cottages and churches as well as for sculpting figurines for roadside shrines and church altars. Similar forms and treatment of the material are encountered on both sides of the Carpathian Mts. – the northern, Slovak, and the southern, Polish side. The distinctive features of a highlander's house include its harmonious plan, perfect proportions, and

■■ **Łopuszna.**
Wooden church
from the turn of
the 15th century.

■■ **Dębno.**
Wooden church
of the Archangel
Michael with
preserved original
painted decoration.

the pleasing natural colour of the wooden walls and shingle roof. A cohesive complex of such buildings has been preserved in the village of Chochołów, to the west of Zakopane. The exceptional beauty of rural church architecture remains the supreme achievement of the highland carpenters. High shingle roofs with ave-bells and defensive shingle-covered turrets facing the west, with an added ice-breaker, resemble Gothic brick architecture. The church in Dębno, one of the oldest wooden churches in the region, was erected in the second half of the 15th century. It is famous for ornate carpentry and especially the almost totally preserved polychrome from the turn of that century, consisting of geometrical, floral-plant, architectural, animal and figurative motifs, such as St. George and the dragon or knights setting off for a hunt. The main altar contains a painted triptych from the early 16th century, typical of the decorative arts of Little Poland. The original wooden tabernacle

with Gothic motifs comes from the same period. The oldest known surviving panel painting in Poland – part of a 13th-century altar with a depiction of two saints – was discovered at Dębno. The interior is additionally embellished with sculptures executed by a local craftsman. The unusually rich and colourful combination of folk and professional art lends a truly remarkable atmosphere of festive joy. (P. T.)

The Pieniny Mts., a small limestone chain, are renowned for wonderful scenery, the outcome of exceptionally variegated relief. The entrance to the Pieniny Mts. was guarded by two castles: Czorsztyn and Niedzica, former border strongholds along a trade route from Poland to Hungary and the meeting place of diplomats from both countries. The 13th-century Polish fortress of Czorsztyn Castle was expanded by Kazimierz the Great during the 14th century. Destroyed in a fire at the end of the 18th

on the left:

■ **Podhale region.**
Chochołów:
19th - century
wooden village
development.

■ **Łopuszna.**
The Tetmajer
manor house,
end of the 18th
century.

century, it was never rebuilt. Niedzica Castle, on the right bank of the River Dunajec, was erected by Hungarian magnates at the beginning of the 14th century. It passed back and forth between Hungarian and Polish lords, and in the 16th century it served for a time as the seat of robber knights. In 1945, the castle came into the possession of the Polish state. As a result of its 17th-century enlargement it consisted of the Gothic upper castle, in ruins today, and the lower castle, rebuilt in the Renaissance style, which houses a retreat for art historians.

The abundant vegetation of the Pieniny Mts. consists of fir and beech forests, covering the mountain slopes and interspersed with larch and yew trees. The mountain meadows are replete with luxuriant grasses and flowers. The warm limestone rocks preserved relics of Tertiary vegetation represented by the fragrant Zawadzki chrysanthemum. The highest and most varied part of the Pieniny Mts. is the Trzy Korony (Three Crowns) massif, the main peak of which is Mt. Okrąglica (982 m), a magnificent viewpoint overlooking the Dunajec Gorge. The river crosses the Pieniny Mts. in a narrow and deep valley, forming an arc with seven, 9 km-long meanders. The Dunajec Gorge is considered to be one of the most beautiful in Europe; floating the rapids on rafts made of dugouts bound together remains a unique experience. The river is also known for sudden rises in the water level which cause flooding. Reservoirs have been built in Rożnów and Czchów in order to regulate the flow of the Dunajec (and to provide electricity). Unfortunately, an electric plant constructed during the 1990s near Czorsztyn together with a complex of dams and reservoirs has seriously changed the local landscape and natural environment.

The Pieniny National Park was founded in 1954 to protect the exceptional landscape of the mountains. The varied relief, interesting rugged crags, the beautiful Dunajec Gorge, and flower-dotted meadows are the reason why the Park is considered to be one of Poland's most attractive tourist spots. (I. J. K.)

North of the Pieniny Mts. lie the Beskidy Mts. To the south-west, the boundary peak is Wielka Racza

on the left:

**Pieniny Mts.
Niedzica Castle.**

(1 236 m), part of a mountain group comprising the Żywiecki Beskid Mts. The forests of Mt. Wielka Racza include beautiful, extensive clearings which offer excellent conditions for skiing. The ski run down the western slope of the mountain to the Slovak side is considered one of the best in the Beskidy Mts. The Śląski Beskid Mts., the most westerly part of the Beskidy Mts., consists of the Czantoria chain and the Barania Góra group. The Czantoria chain is lower and its slopes are more corrugated; the highest peak is Czantoria Wielka (995 m). Mt. Skrzyczne, the main peak in the Barania Góra group, rises to an altitude of 1 257 m, and Mt. Barania Góra itself is 1 220 m high. Its slopes are the site of the headsprings of the Biała and Czarna Wisełka, which merge to create the Vistula. The Barania Góra group is a popular tourist and vacation area, visited in particular by the inhabitants of the nearby Upper Silesian Basin. The best known resorts include Wisła, Brenna, Bystra, Szczyrk, Jaszowiec and Ustroń. The village of Koniaków, famed for its handmade lace, lies in a depression between the Silesian and Żywiecki Beskid Mts. This rare craft has been also mastered by the women of Istebna, another village of the region. The inhabitants of both villages wear their regional costumes daily. Many localities in the Beskidy highlands have preserved rich folklore in unique architecture, carvings, paintings, music, dances and colourful dress. (I. J. K.)

The town of Wadowice is located at the foot of the Mały Beskid Mts. on the River Skawa, a tributary of

on the left:

**Trzy Korony -
highest massif
in the Pieniny Mts.**

on pages 42-43:

**Beskid Makowski
Mts.**

**Beskid Śląski.
The river Biała
Wisełka.**

Bernardine monastery founded by him in 1602, and continues to fulfil this function to the present day. The originally Mannerist monastery buildings, erected from 1603 to 1609, were later redesigned in the Baroque style; to the north and east they are surrounded by 42 Calvary chapels built on hillocks and in hollows (17th-19th century). A Holy Week mystery play – the Way of the Cross – is enacted annually by the inhabitants of neighbouring villages, a tradition that dates back to the18th century. (I. J. K.)

The town of Lanckorona features a historic urban layout and a characteristic complex of 19th-century wooden town buildings. The market square and several streets display picturesque ground-floor buildings with gables facing the street. High shingle roofs include markedly projecting eaves, arranged in picturesque rows.

The highest rise in the Beskid Mts. is the Babia Góra range. This asymmetrical massif is composed of steep northern faces, rocky in places and crossed by numerous stream valleys, and southern, gently descending slopes. The highest peak, Mt. Babia Góra (1 725 m), has a rocky summit called "Diablak," covered with rock debris. The slopes of Mt. Babia Góra are richly forested up to an altitude of 1 400 m: fir and beech to 1 150 m, and spruce above. Dwarf mountain pines and flower-strewn meadows stretch higher up (to 1 650 m). The Babia Góra National Park was set up to protect this primeval natural environment. (I. J. K.)

Picturesque Nowy Wiśnicz Castle, located on a wooded hillock over the Leksandrówka river valley, was built in the second half of the 14th century. The whole region belonged to a powerful local family. In the first half of the 15th century, its last representative, Piotr Kmita III, redesigned the stronghold into an imposing residence. At the end of the 16th century, the castle became the property of the Lubomirskis. In 1616, Stanisław Lubomirski, the voivode of Cracow, founded the town of Wiśnicz

Wadowice. Family home of Pope John Paul II.

the Vistula; this railway and road junction has been a industrial centre (processing) since the 19th century. Already during the 16th century, Wadowice was known for a school run by the burghers. The town became truly famous in 1978 when Karol Wojtyła, born and brought up in Wadowice, was elected Pope John Paul II. The Pope's birth and christening are registered in the former parish church, rebuilt in the Baroque style at the end of the 18th century. The Wojtyła family home has been adapted to serve as a museum dedicated to the Holy Father.

on the right:

Parish church of the Presentation of the Holy Virgin Mary.

Kalwaria Zebrzydowska, situated between the Makowski Beskid Mts. and the Wielki (Great) Foothills, was established in 1617 by Mikołaj Zebrzydowski, the voivode of Cracow, as a pilgrim centre attached to a

Nowy and erected a Carmelite church and monastery on a hill facing the castle. The castle was remodelled between 1615 and 1621. At that time, all the Lubomirski buildings were designed by the Italian architect Matteo Trapola, an original albeit indecisive architect whose vacillation between Mannerist tradition and Baroque innovations is exemplified by the interesting entrance gate. The castle and monastery were surrounded with typical Italian fortifications, including regular pentagonal bastions. The loggia in the castle's small inner courtyard, the chapel, and the residential annex with a main hall supported on two pillars, were probably also conceived by Trapola. Lubomirski was an acclaimed collector and patron of the arts: the earliest performances of Italian opera in Poland were staged at Wiśnicz. During the 17th century, the invading Swedish army pillaged nearly fifty cartloads of valuable furniture, tapestries and paintings. The castle, which belonged successively to the Sanguszko, Potocki and Zamoyski families, was inhabited until 1780 and underwent restoration in 1909 and 1928. Basic restoration was inaugurated after the second world war. The interiors have retained few traces of the castle's former glory; parts of the original stucco designed by J. C. Falconi have survived as well as fragments of polychrome in the chapel and assorted rooms, as well as Early Baroque fireplaces and portals.

During the Late Middle Ages, Lipnica Murowana, located on a busy trail to Hungary, was a prosperous small town, as witnessed by three local churches. The cemetery church of St. Leonard, constructed in the second half of the 15th century, is one of the oldest examples of wooden sacral architecture in Little Poland. Its nave is surrounded with open arcades (*soboty*) designed to protect the congregation against inclement weather. The interior features polychrome decorations and three Late Gothic triptychs.

Nowy Sącz, at the confluence of the Kamienica and Dunajec rivers, is the capital of the Sącz region, founded as a royal defensive town in 1292 by Wenceslas II, King of Bohemia and Poland. During the 14th century, Kazimierz the Great erected a cas-

tle and encircled the town with walls. Location on a prominent trade route with Hungary favoured rapid development – the town prospered and became a centre of the crafts. A parish school was established early in the 15th century. Jan Długosz, a fifteenth-century historian, diplomat, royal canon and personal tutor to the sons of King Kazimierz Jagiellon, wrote his history of Poland while residing in Nowy Sącz. Here Michał Sędziwój (Sendivogius Polonus), an alchemist of European renown and the acknowledged keeper of the secret of the philosophical stone, wrote an alchemical treatise, later translated into numerous languages (53 editions between 1604 and 1797). The golden age in Nowy Sącz's economic and cultural history ended with the first Swedish invasion ("deluge") of Poland in the mid-17th century.

Lipnica Murowana.
Church of St.
Leonard.

on the left:

Nowy Wiśnicz.
Castle.

on pages 48-49:

View from Mt.
Jaworzyna Krynicka.

Cieszyn.
Romanesque rotunda
of St. Nicholas,
11th century.

on the right:

Nowy Sącz.
Town hall from
1895-1897.

Nowy Sącz was spared the total destruction planned by the Germans when the castle, where explosives were stored and a Nazi sapper detachment stationed, was blown up. Despite numerous wartime conflagrations and losses Nowy Sącz can still boast of historic monuments from assorted periods, starting with those dating back to the Middle Ages (the Gothic Franciscan friary and collegiate churches). Another historic town is Stary Sącz, lying in the fork of the Poprad and Dunajec rivers and recorded as a castellan castle-town already in 1224. It too belonged to a system of fortified towns guarding the "Hungarian" route; during the 14th-16th century Stary Sącz prospered from the grain and wine trade, and became one of the wealthiest Carpathian boroughs. The Swedish deluge (second half of the 17th century) arrested all development, and the town gradualy declined. During the 18th century, a local Poor Clare convent opened the first Polish school for "lay girls". Today, the town of Stary Sącz, brimming with historical monuments, lies on the fringe of a vast fruit-growing area, whose centre is Łącko. The apple orchards number several score thousand trees, and every May Łącko organises the "Blossoming Apple Tree" festival. The local plum brandy has also won wide acclaim.

The Beskid Sądecki Mts., divided by the Poprad river valley into two ranges: the Radziejowa and the Jaworzyna, lie to the south of Stary Sącz. Sunny alpine meadows stretch below lofty peaks and intriguing rock formations. Numerous health resorts and spas, famed for their mineral waters, include Żegiestów on the southern slopes of the Poprad valley, as well as Muszyna and Piwniczna, also on the Poprad. Szczawnica, in the picturesque Grajcarek valley between the Pieniny Mts. and the Beskid Sądecki Mts., evolved into a spa already in the second half of the 19th century. The most popular and largest resort is Krynica, known as "the pearl of Polish spas". Mineral springs abound, including the "Zuber", one of the most plentiful acidulous-alkaline springs in Europe. The medicinal properties of the Krynica springs were discovered at the end of the 18th century. The rapid advancement of the spa

Military operations, plunder, fires and epidemics caused widespread destruction and casualties. At the time of a rebellion against the Swedes, which broke out in 1655, Nowy Sącz was among the first Polish towns to recover freedom, albeit it never regained its former status and experienced prolonged economic stagnation. Not until the second half of the 19th century did a new era of urban expansion dawn with the opening of a railway line and the ensuing development of the machine-building, food processing, chemical and wood industries. During the Nazi occupation, the town was an important centre for the Polish Resistance, which used it for the conveyance of people across the border to Hungary. One-third of the population was exterminated by the Nazis or died as a result of German reprisal. In January 1945,

Lake Rożnowskie. started in the second half of the last century, and continues up to this day. The town has preserved examples of old wooden architecture and Art Nouveau sanatoria. The celebrated naive painter Nikifor (1895-1968) resided and worked in Krynica. The regional spas also operate as tourist centres; the natural beauty of the Beskid Sądecki Mts., which offer breathtaking views, create ideal conditions for repose, hiking and skiing. (I. J. K.)

Wooden churches encountered on the Beskidy slopes are traces of the shepherds and farmers who until recently inhabited the Beskid foothills and who were the followers of Eastern Christianity. These monuments comprise the most westward examples of

eastern Slavonic culture. Derived from Byzantine tradition, in the course of centuries the buildings succumbed to the influence of Western monumental architecture, reflected in the Gothic solid and the Baroque bell-tower cupolas and interiors, although external impact was adapted to the construction potential of wooden architecture. Monuments of sacral architecture in Powroźnik (1643), Wojkowa (1790) and Dubne (1863) are examples of the Uniate churches built by the Łemko people of the Sub-Carpathian region, who preserved the liturgy. At first glance, these shingle churches, with slender towers built facing the west and surrounded by old trees, appear to resemble the Catholic village churches of the region. Examined from the east, they disclose

specific towering solids composed of three distinct parts: the presbytery, the nave and the tower, rising above the porch. This uniqueness is also accentuated by the pavilion roofs, which create a pyramid whose sophisticated forms and proportions are the work of rural carpenters. The interior consisted of a porch intended for women (*babiniec*), a nave designed for men, and a presbytery separated from the nave by an iconostasis. The façades of the Łemko churches and cottages were usually painted, the dominating colours being deep red, navy blue and ochre. Unfortunately, little of the original hues has remained. The shingle roofs are increasingly replaced with tin, frequently simplifying the complex line of the structures by reducing the number of

mansards. This exceptionally interesting group of architectural monuments, unique on a European scale and the product of a junction between the East and the West, is slowly decaying. (P. T.)

One of the most charming and ancient towns of the Sub-Carpathian region is Biecz, located on the steep bank of the River Ropa, and in the past known as "little Cracow". During the 14th and 16th century, Biecz prospered thanks to trade with Hungary, as evidenced by an extant bastion, a remnant of the town defence walls, a town hall with a Late Gothic turret, and a monumental parish church from 1516-1521. The church interior has retained many valuable works of art, including a painting from the school of

Tylicz. Wooden Uniate church of the Łemko people, built in 1738-1744.

on the right:

Biecz.
Parish church of
Corpus Christi.

Michelangelo and a carved Renaissance music stand. Sanok, one of the oldest towns along the trade route with Hungary, was mentioned in documents from the mid-12th century. In 1344, King Kazimierz the Great incorporated the town into the Crown and erected a castle and defensive fortifications. Today, the castle houses a Historical Museum featuring the most valuable collection of icons in Poland (14th-19th century). The Museum of Folk Architecture of the eastern Sub-Carpathian region, once inhabited by such ethnic groups as the Łemko, Bojko and Pogórzanie people, was opened in 1958. More than seventy wooden structures are displayed in an area of 26 hectares: cottages, entire farmsteads, farm buildings and Uniate churches with preserved interiors, the oldest originating from the 18th century. Earliest mention of Dukla, a town situated in the Beskid Niski Mts., is to be found in historical documents from the second half of the 14th century. The settlement, conveniently located along the aforementioned trade route with Hungary, was granted municipal status in 1380. The interior of the local parish church from 1764-1765, with typically Rococo decoration, represents superior artistic merits. The sepulchral chamber of Amelia Mniszech, born Brühl, who died in 1772, is particularly interesting. The designer, probably Jan Obrocki, granted the sepulchre the shape and ambience of a palatial Rococo boudoir. The figure of the deceased reclines on a black marble socle standing in a sophisticated interior containing great mirrors; the overall effect is of slumber which had interrupted the enjoyment of a fashionable novel. The sculptor achieved an extraordinary depiction of the intricate folds and frills of the exquisite, flowing gown. The whole composition is associated with the magnificent achievements of the Rococo-era Lvov school.

A conspicuous example of wooden church architecture is the three-nave church in the village of Szalowa, erected in 1739-1756. The originality of the monument lies in an attempt to emulate monumental, Late Baroque architecture. The colourful and stylistically uniform interior from the mid-1700s blends Baroque and Rococo forms as well as the traditions of folk and professional art.

on pages 56-57:

Bieszczady Mts.
Wetlińska Połonina.

Sanok. Museum of Folk Architecture.

on the right:

Bieszczady Mts. Smolnik, Uniate church of the Archangel Michael from 1791.

The unspoilt natural beauty of the Bieszczady Mts., Poland's most peripheral mountain group, attracts increasing numbers of visitors. The main bases for excursions are located in Ustrzyki Górne, Cisna and Komańcza; the wooden Uniate church in the latter locality was constructed in 1805. Of all the Beskid ranges only the Bieszczady Mts. lack the upper level forest; their uppermost parts are overgrown with tall grasses, abundant flowers, and alder shrubs. These extensive meadows, known as *połoniny*, offer excellent visibility and in winter become superb ski slopes. The best known *połoniny* – Caryńska and Wetlińska – have been used as grazing grounds; today, they have been partially incorporated into the Bieszczady National Park. The lower terrain is covered with beech forests or mixed fir and beech woods, with a thick undergrowth. The exceptionally low upper limit of the woodlands does not exceed 1 200 m. The steep mountain slopes are crossed by rapid mountain streams which flow to the River San. The Bieszczady Mts., a western branch of the Eastern Carpathian Mts., consist of long parallel ridges divided by wide depressions. The highest peaks in the Polish part of the range are Mt. Tarnica (1 346 m) and the neighbouring summits of Krzemień and Halicz, both rising to a height of 1 335 m. The some-

**Krynica.
The Old Pump-room.**

on the right:

**Bieszczady Mts.
Komańcza. Wooden
Uniate church of Our
Lady of Custody,
built at the
beginning of the
19th century.**

what lower Wielka Rawka (1 304 m) constitutes the main mountaintop of a ridge forming the border between Poland, Ukraine and Slovakia. Prior to the second world war, the Bieszczady Mts. were a densely populated agricultural region. At the time of the battles waged against the Ukrainian nationalists in 1944-1947, the majority of the settlements was burned down and part of the population was resettled, either to the Soviet Union or Polish western territories. The only vestiges of some of the villages are solitary houses or churches. Consequently, tourism in this almost uninhabited terrain originally assumed the form of expeditions to a virgin land. A resettlement and development programme was initiated in the 1950s, but the Bieszczady Mts. still remain one of the most sparsely populated areas in Poland. Settlements concentrate in the valleys and wide depressions between the ridges. The local populace subsists mainly on forestry and shepherding. Sheep are transported from the Podhale region and the Wesern Beskidy Mts. for summer grazing. The Bieszczady Mts. remain predominantly a haven for tourists. Magnificent scenery together with attractive, exotic terrains draw increasing numbers of

sightseers, some of whom seek distant camping sites while the majority set off on excursions from villages lying at the foot of the mountains. Man still remains little more than a guest in these hills, and rarely ventures into the wilderness beyond the marked trails.The animal life of the Bieszczady forests includes deer, wild boar and the specially introduced European bison; pride of place goes to the local wolf, lynx and bear, and among the birds – to the golden eagle. Venomous snakes abound. Bountiful wildlife attracts hunters, particularly in winter. (I. J. K.)

The greatest tourist attraction in the lower, less forested and more densely populated northern Bieszczady Foothills is Lake Solina, created in 1968 after the construction of a dam and a hydroelectric power plant on the River San near Lesko. Although the area (21 sq. km) of the lake comes sixth among Poland's artificial reservoirs, it is the deepest (82 m) and holds the greatest volume of water (506 mln. cu.m). The location of Lake Solina amidst picturesque hills enhances its appeal as a tourist and water sports centre. Modern hotels and camping sites have mushroomed on the lake shores. Solina and the resort of Polańczyk are the most popular local tourist centres. The smaller Myczkowskie Lake, with a recreation centre in Myczkowce, stretches below the Solina dam. (I. J. K.)

Krasiczyn lies on the right bank of the San, in the Przemyśl Foothills. When in 1598 Marcin Krasicki, the voivode of Podolia and a count of the Holy Roman Empire, became the owner of Krasiczyn, he embarked on rebuilding the late mediaeval castle into an extensive residence around a rectangular courtyard. Italian architects designed a Mannerist castle, suffused with symbolic contents. Krasicki probably intended his residence to reflect the then recognised theoretical hierarchy of the world, cultivated by the Polish gentry; hence, the four corner bastions were named Divine (Boska), Papal (Papieska), Royal (Królewska) and Noble (Szlachecka), with suitably adapted forms of the cupolas and attics, colourful sgraffito decorations on the outer walls,

and assorted functions (for example, the Divine Tower contained a chapel). The façade of Krasiczyn Castle is adorned with busts of Roman emperors, Biblical scenes, portraits of Polish monarchs and figures of knights and saints. Each wing was given an attic of different design, and the courtyard was encircled with ground-floor galleries. Greatest destruction was caused by a fire in 1852 and the events of the first world war. Extensive conservation was inaugurated at the beginning of the 1970s. The steep escarpment of the San is also the site of the picturesquely situated town of Przemyśl, together with its historic Old Town. The earliest record of Przemyśl comes from 981, and the golden age of the town spanned from the 15th to the 17th century; this is also the period of the origin of its historical monuments. The local museums feature valuable

Przemyśl.
Cathedral of St. John
the Baptist.

on the left:

Krasiczyn.
View of castle
bastions: Boska
(in background)
and Szlachecka.

collections of icons and tapestries. Together with the close-by town of Jarosław, Przemyśl was located along the busy trade route to Rus' and Hungary. During the 16th and 17th century, the local merchants built arcaded town houses modelled on Italian residences, of which the most magnificent preserved example, with an expanded attic, was erected in Jarosław by the Orsettis, an Italian merchant family. Leżajsk, whose history dates back to ancient Slav days, lies in the valley of the Lower San. The town is a celebrated pilgrimage centre – the local Marian cult concentrates around a painting of the Madonna and Child displayed in the Bernardine church (first half of the 17th century). The same church houses a magnificent organ designed after 1678 and spanning three naves. The motifs of the exceptionally elaborate carved decoration of the organ comprise an apotheosis of the Church, the mission of the Holy Virgin Mary, the patron saint of the order, in the redemption of mankind, and the battle waged by Hercules against a hydra – a symbol of the struggle conducted during the Counter-Reformation by the Catholic Church against dissidents. This striking work is extremely Polish in its striving towards

Jarosław.
The Orsetti House.

on the left:

Jarosław.
Town hall redesigned
in 1895-1896 in the
Neo-Renaissance
style.

on pages 66-67:

Łańcut. Palace, front
elevation.

**Rzeszów.
The Lubomirski
Castle.**

astounding dimension and opulence. The foremost historical monument in Łańcut is the Early Baroque palace constructed in 1629-1641 by the architect Matteo Trapola around a square courtyard and including four corner towers and bastille fortification. Today, the palace, redesigned upon several occasions and surrounded by a picturesque landscape, acts as a museum of interiors and a background for numerous cultural events, primarily music festivals. (P. T.)

The castle in Baranów Sandomierski was built for the Leszczyński family at the turn of the 16th century, probably in accordance with a project by Santi Gucci, the Florentine architect and sculptor who redesigned the earlier defensive manor house. The castle represents a synthesis of an arcaded courtyard residence, patterned after the Royal Castle on Wawel Hill in Cracow and employing Mannerist solutions. Santi Gucci, who came to Poland at the beginning of the 1550s, introduced Florentine forms of sophisticated Mannerism. His status as a royal court artist,

on the right:
**Leżajsk.
Early Baroque
Bernardine church
(built in 1618-1628).**

on the right:

Baranów Sandomierski. Castle courtyard with arcades.

together with an opportunity to lease the stone quarry in Pińczów, enabled him to pursue an ambitious building and sculptural programme, continued by associates after his death in 1600. The castle was erected on a regular plan with corner towers lending it a defensive character. The façade with an expanded attic constitutes a blank wall – a screen enclosing the courtyard. The unexpected effects typical of Mannerism include an entrance gate which is impassable and conceals a staircase to the raised courtyard. Carved portals, characteristic for the Gucci workshop, lead to the first-storey chambers. Today, the beautiful courtyard is the site of frequent concerts and theatrical events. The castle contains the Museum of the Sulphur Basin. (P. T.)

The late mediaeval town of Tarnów, which flourished during the 15th and 16th centuries, is rich in preserved art treasures from bygone days. The Gothic town hall was redesigned in the second half of the 16th century, and assumed the shape of a Late Renaissance edifice. Its expanded attic, inspired by the Cracow Cloth Hall, was outfitted with gargoyles. The Gothic cathedral contains Mannerist chapels and tombs. In 1561-1567, Giovanni Maria Mosca of Padua, the Italian sculptor known as Padovano, who worked in Poland since 1532, installed in the presbytery wall a stately tombstone of Hetman Jan Tarnowski. After the death in 1567 of his son, Jan Krzysztof, the tombstone was raised and transformed into a two-level object. The architectural mounting refers to Venetian models, and the composition is typical for two-level tombstones, extremely common in Poland during the 16th century and the first half of the 17th century, with slumbering figures – portraits of the deceased – patterned on the humanistic artworks of the Italian Renaissance. The likenesses are accompanied by personifications of virtues: Justice, Prudence, Victory and Glory. The Diocesan Museum, located in a complex of mediaeval town houses next to the cathedral, features remarkable collections of late mediaeval paintings and sculptures from Little Poland, whose value is second only to the exhibits displayed in Cracow. (P. T.)

The village of Zalipie near Dąbrowa Tarnowska is a well-known centre of folk art. Traditional folk painting, which almost disappeared in the 19th century, was revived during the inter-war period by the local village women. Upon the initiative of Felicja Curyłowa, the farmers' wives began painting the framework of their cottages and adorning the interiors with plant motifs. A folk art museum was organised in Curyłowa's cottage after her death in 1974. (I. J. K.)

The town of Wieliczka lies along the border between the Wieliczka and Bochnia Foothills. The original ancient settlement was created next to saltworks

mines. The presence of salt beds stimulated the further development of Wieliczka, as testified by the original name of the settlement: Wielka Sól (Magnum Sal). Salt mining in Wieliczka dates back to at least the 9th century, and its expansion is associated with Kinga, the wife of Duke Bolesław the Chaste (1226-1279); the mine itself, which was royal property, was leased to magnates. Following the first partition of Poland (1772), the mine passed into Austrian hands; since 1918, it has belonged to the Polish state. Today, salt continues to be extracted in certain parts of the mine while others have been turned into a Museum of the Cracow Salt Mines encompassing, i.a.

Village of Zalipie.
Decorated cottage.

on the left:
Tarnów.
Cathedral of the
Nativity of the Holy
Virgin Mary.

unused chambers with galleries carved in salt, spell-binding corridors and halls, as well as the St. Antho-ny and Holy Cross chapels, designed in the 17th century, and the Blessed Kinga chapel (19th centu-ry), embellished with bas-reliefs. The exhibits include numerous sculptures and statues of saints and miners carved out of salt. The museum traces the history of salt mining and features equipment, tools and transport facilities from the Middle Ages on. Some of the chambers are used for therapeutic purposes. The Crystal Grottoes – natural rock vacu-ums – discovered during the exploitation of salt, have been placed under strict protection. Their walls are covered with salt crystals about 10 cm long; exceptional specimen attain a length of 46 cm.
In 1978, the Wieliczka salt mine was registered on the UNESCO world cultural legacy list. (I. J. K.)

Oświęcim, a town with a rich and tragic history, is situated almost in the centre of the Oświęcim Basin, on the right bank of the Soła at its outlet to the Vistula. As early as 1150 it was marked on a map drawn by the Arabian scholar al Idrisi as an impor-tant stronghold on the route from Rus' to Silesia and Moravia. From 1317, Oświęcim was the capital of a separate duchy, which in 1456 was purchased by King Kazimierz Jagiellon and in 1564 became incorporated into the Crown as part of the Cracow voivodeship. During the Reformation, the borough was the scene of turbulent religious clashes. After the first partition (1772), it was annexed by Austria. A small industrial and trading town before the se-cond world war, it is now an important industrial and communication centre. The name Oświęcim is linked, above all, with the largest World War II concentration camp established in 1940 during the Nazi occupation. Konzentrationslager Auschwitz-Birkenau was one of the most appalling death camps in which millions of people of 28 nationalities lost their lives, primarily Jews, Gypsies and Poles. In memory of their martyrdom, the whole camp has been turned into a museum. A specially constructed monument commemorates victims of the Nazi exter-mination policy. (I. J. K.)

on the left:

Oświęcim. Gate of the Auschwitz-Birkenau death camp.

Uplands

The rich natural resources of the Silesian Upland led to the creation of the biggest mining and heavy industry district in Poland. The first written records of mining in Upper Silesia date back to the 12th century; it is known, however, that the mining and smelting of silver, lead and iron ores started much earlier, and only the exploitation of zinc ore was initiated as late as the 18th century. The development of mining and industry was primarily connected with coal. It was precisely in Silesia that two blast furnaces fired with coke, the first ones in Europe, were constructed at the turn of the 18th century. The growing importance of coal during the 19th century was the reason for the concentration of industry within the coal basin and the spontaneous growth of towns. Villages turned into workers' settlements and new townships arose and merged with old urban centres. Gradually, the area of the central coal basin became a gigantic urban-industrial complex known as the Upper Silesian Industrial District (Górnośląski Okręg Przemysłowy – GOP), in which coal mining continues to play the foremost role. As a rule, Silesia brings to mind the splendid gala uniforms worn by the miners on special occasions. Silesian folk costumes are less well known, although those from the region of Dąbrówka Wielka are particularly interesting.

The main cultural and economic centre of the GOP is located in Katowice, whose advancement was linked, above all, with the growing significance attached to coal mining. One of the oldest mines is "Kleofas", working since 1822. Katowice was granted municipal status in 1865. Inferior workers' districts, which emerged in the vicinity of the mines and factories, were partially replaced by modern housing estates.

on the right:

Olsztyn (Częstochowa Upland). Ruins of castle.

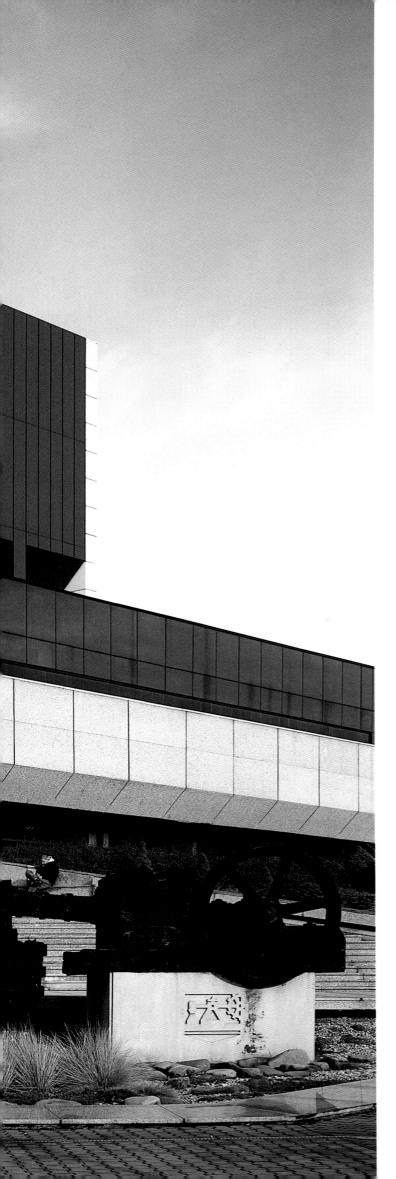

The city centre was also redesigned. The heavy concentration of industry in the GOP has brought about detrimental changes of the natural environment. No other part of Poland is so affected by the economy. Intensive mining, heavy industry and urban development have totally transformed the natural environment, including water, soil and vegetation. The landscape is dominated by smoking chimneys, blast furnaces, lift shafts, spoil banks and swallow holes created by mining. The densely populated region suffers from chronic shortages of water, which is polluted anyway. Countermeasures aimed against air pollution have been introduced in the form of new city parks, recultivated spoil banks and workings, artificial reservoirs, etc. A protective forest belt has been planted around the Upper Silesian agglomeration. New housing estates have been built beyond the coal basin. It was decided to limit the expansion of industrial enterprises not directly connected with coal mining, or to locate them outside the basin, as in the case of the electric power station in Łaziska Górne and the "Katowice" steelworks. The most interesting cultural centres and museums in Katowice include the Polish Stage Design Centre, a department of the Silesian Museum. The Centre specialises in collecting projects of sets, costumes and props devised by such outstanding Polish artists as A. Wajda, O. Axer and A. Kilian. Attention is due to the Silesian Library, the largest institution of its sort in Poland; housed in a modern building on Rada Europy (Council of Europe) Square, it amasses bibliophile and unique editions, as well as the underground press and publications issued outside the range of official censorship in the 1970s and 1980s. The industrial centres of the Upper Silesian Industrial District include numerous old towns featuring assorted historical monuments. One such town is Będzin, on the Cracow-Wrocław route trade, which evolved from a settlement at the foot of a 13th-century Gothic castle with a tower from the turn of the 13th century. Today, the castle, partially reconstructed after the second world war, houses the Dąbrowa Basin Museum.

on the left:

Katowice.

The Silesian Library.

Pszczyna.
Fragment of interior.

on the right:

Pszczyna. Palace.

The town of Pszczyna lies beyond the Upper Silesian agglomeration, albeit still within the range of the voivodeship of Silesia. A former ducal seat, Pszczyna has expanded to become an industry and service centre. A settlement was probably established here in the 10th century; its numerous owners included the dukes of Racibórz, members of the Jagiellonian royal dynasty, the Cieszyn Piasts and the German Hochbergs von Pless. Pszczyna returned to Poland in 1921, and during the inter-war period the princes, owners of vast landed estates, coal mines and factories, were known to be among the richest families in Europe. The Gothic castle, erected on the site of a castle-town, was completely rebuilt between 1743 and 1767, and again in 1870-1874. A museum of richly outfitted period interiors, exhibiting various examples of 19th-century stylisation maintained in the spirit of past epochs, was opened in 1945.

The castle is set amidst the loveliest park in Silesia, recognised as a natural reserve of ancient trees and rare species of plants. The Pszczyna woods contain a reservation of European bisons, established in 1865 (in the village of Jankowice). (I. J. K.)

Częstochowa, situated in the northern part of the Silesian Upland, was created in 1826 out of two towns – Stara Częstochowa on the River Warta and Częstochówka, lying at the foot of the Jasna Góra hill. The settlements were first mentioned in 1220. In 1356, Częstochowa was granted a *locatio* privilege, while a document issued in 1377 by Duke Władysław II Opolczyk, who conferred ironworks to his brothers, Jaśko and Niczko, referred to Stara Częstochowa as a town. Five years later, the Duke brought over from Hungary members of the Paulite order, endowing them with a monastery raised next to the church on Jasna Góra. The same year, the monastery church received a painting of the Most Holy Virgin Mary, probably of Byzantine origin, which became renowned for its miraculous properties and up to this day draws pilgrims from all over Poland. The monastery was successively rebuilt, and in 1620 it was strongly fortified according to innovative designs introduced from Italy. The protective functions of the mighty Częstochowa fortifications were displayed most famously during the Swedish invasion of 1655, when a small group of defenders succeeded in repulsing the attacks of the vastly superior forces of the enemy regular army. Annual pilgrimages greatly influenced the local crafts: the settlement of Częstochówka developed largely in order to serve the needs of the pilgrims. It achieved municipal status in 1717 when it began to be known as Nowa Częstochowa. Industry progressed in unified Częstochowa during the last three decades of the 19th century, and was particularly expanded after the second world war, when the town became one of the most important industrial centres in Poland. Textile manufacturing and metallurgy lead the field, perpetuating old local traditions; numerous plants specialise in other branches. The city continued to grow and new housing estates appeared

on the left:

Częstochowa.
Monastery
on Jasna Góra.

on the right:

**Podzamcze.
Ogrodzieniec Castle,
view from the east.**

together with two higher education institutes. Częstochowa – the site of the best known Polish sanctuary – is a prominent tourist centre. The Jasna Góra monastery, a monument of national culture and the largest religious cult centre, annually attracts millions of pilgrims and visitors. The originally Gothic monastery, having undergone a number of additions and conversions, is predominantly Baroque, as is a large part of its richly decorated interiors. The numerous historical objects include particularly noteworthy and valuable examples of goldsmithery displayed in the monastery treasury, book and archival collections, and an 18th-century printing house. (I. J. K.)

Numerous watch towers and fortified castles constructed during the reign of Kazimierz the Great on the craggy limestone hills of the Cracow-Częstochowa Upland guarded the border with Silesia, which had been lost to Bohemia. Today, an attractive tourist route known as the Eagle Nest Trail winds through the hills for about 160 km. Apart from the picturesque limestone residual rocks, the route offers historic monuments and natural sights. The majority of the castles is in ruins, primarily as the outcome of the 17th-century Swedish wars.

The highest elevation in the Upland (Mt. Zamkowa, 504 m) is crowned with the magnificent Gothic and Renaissance ruins of Ogrodzieniec Castle, constructed in 1530-1545 for Seweryn Boner, banker to King Zygmunt the Old. The castle, superbly merged with the rocky base, was burned by the Swedes and subsequently partly rebuilt. It remained in a relatively good state until the 19th century when, abandoned, it fell into ruin; ultimately, it was totally devastated during the second world war. Work on protecting the ruins was conducted in 1949-1973. Recently, the castle served as a setting for Andrzej Wajda's film *Zemsta (Revenge)*.

on pages 86-87:

**Mirów. Ruins of one
of the fortresses in
the Cracow-Częstochowa
Upland.**

Ojców and its environs, now a national park, and particularly the steep gorge of the Prądnik valley, are considered to be the most beautiful part of the Cracow-Częstochowa Upland. In the upper part of the Prądnik valley stands Pieskowa Skała (Dog's Rock)

Rudno. Tenczyn Castle.

Castle, built during the 14th century by Kazimierz the Great on a rocky promontory. Originally a Gothic structure, the castle, one of the most magnificent in Poland, was redesigned during the 16th century to become a Renaissance residence of the Szafraniec family. Following the ravages caused by the Swedish wars, the castle was rebuilt by the Zebrzydowski family. Towards the close of the 19th century, Pieskowa Skała, supposedly gambled away in a card game, was purchased with public donations and adapted for use as a holiday hotel. Restored in 1960-1970, the castle houses valuable art collections. The building consists of several sections, with extant Gothic parts; the arcaded courtyard is the most impressive feature. Below the castle rises the famous Club of Hercules, a free-standing limestone monadnock.

on the right:

Pieskowa Skała. Castle.

on pages 90-91:

Tyniec. Benedictine Abbey.

The picturesque ruins of a 14th-century castle, once the property of the Tenczyńskis, a powerful family from Little Poland, rise from volcanic rocks near the village of Rudno, at the southern end of the Cracow-Częstochowa Upland. Originally Gothic, the castle was remodelled in 1570 to become a grand Renaiss-

ance residence, used until the 18th century. (I. J. K.)

Tyniec Abbey, a resplendent Benedictine complex, rises above the Vistula on steep limestonerocks in a narrow gorge known as the Cracow Gate, separating the Cracow-Częstochowa Upland and the Sub-Carpathian region. According to the chronicles of Jan Długosz, the abbey was founded by Kazimierz the Restorer in 1044. The abbot of Tyniec was the superior of all the Benedictine monasteries in Poland, Silesia and, later on, Lithuania. During the 15th century, the 11th-century Romanesque basilica, destroyed in 1241 by the Tartars, was replaced by a Gothic church whose walls have been preserved up to this day in an Early Baroque church from 1618-1622. Following the cassation of the Benedictine order in 1817, the abbey was entrusted to the Jesuits; it was restored to the Benedictines before the second world war.

A 17th-century Cameldolite church and monastery complex, surrounded by wood-lands, lies to the east of Tyniec, on Srebrna Skała (Silver Rock) in Bielany, today a district of Cracow.

on the right:

Cracow. Market Square, Cloth Hall.

Cracow, the former capital of Poland, is both a monument to her past and a bustling contemporary city. In ancient days, it was most probably one of the centres of the Wiślanie tribe. The name comes from the legendary Duke Krak, who founded the town having slain a dragon living in Wawel Cave. Legend also recounts the fate of Krak's daughter, Wanda, who preferred to drown in the Vistula to marrying a German lord and surrendering her native land to him. Long before the foundation of the Polish state, the town was preceded by a large stronghold on Wawel Hill. At the time of the first Piast rulers, this was the seat of the ducal court; during the fragmentation of the country into provinces it served the senior duke. After the reunification of Polish lands, Wawel Castle became the abode of Polish monarchs until the late 16th century, and remained a royal residence and a coronation site to the partitions. As early as the 10th century, Cracow, lying at the foot of Wawel Hill, had become a significant populous settlement along a major trade route between the East and Prague. Following its destruction by the Tartars in 1241, the town was completely rebuilt and organised anew according to a *locatio* privilege from 1257. It was at this time that the regular street network of the Old Town was delineated, including the extensive (4 hectares) Market Square, occupied by stalls which during the 14th century were replaced by the Cloth Hall. Burnt down in the 16th century, the Hall was rebuilt with a fine Renaissance attic wall. The only remnant of the 14th century town hall is a lofty, partially reconstructed Gothic tower, which in the 18th century was given a Baroque cupola. One of the corners of the Market Square is occupied by the magnificent Gothic church of the Holy Virgin Mary. The Square also contains two small churches and imposing burghers' houses. (I.J.K.)

In the second half of the 15th century and during the 16th century Cracow flourished as the royal capital of the increasingly powerful Jagiellon monarchy, whose members competed with the Habsburgs for dominance in Eastern and Central Europe. The transference of the Polish capital to Warsaw in 1596,

and the impact of political and economic crises at the turn of the 17th century caused Cracow to lose its former splendour. In 1795, it came under Austrian rule in the wake of the third partition of Poland, and in 1809-1815 the town became part of the Duchy of Warsaw. The Congress of Vienna granted Cracow the status of a free city, but in 1846 it was again incorporated into the Austrian Empire, as reprisal for the so-called Cracow revolution. Transformed into a provincial borough of the Austro-Hungarian monarchy Cracow did not enjoy conditions conducive for economic growth, but it never ceased to remain a powerful centre of Polish national and political life; this holds true particularly for culture and science. The Jagiellonian University, founded in 1364 by Kazimierz the Great, the first academy in Poland and one of Europe's oldest, was attended by Poles from all three partitions. Cracow was the birthplace of new schools of scientific thought, literary trends and styles in art. At the beginning of the 20th century, the "Jama Michalikowa" cafe was a meeting place of artists and writers from all over Poland, while the renowned Słowacki Theatre became a leading Polish dramatic stage. The quickened pace of urban growth in independent Poland was halted by the second world war. Under German occupation, Cracow was turned into the administrative capital of the so-called General Gouvernement. The city was looted, losing many of its treasures. Nazi plans to blow up Wawel Castle and many other historical buildings before retreating were obstructed by a Soviet army manoeuvre which compelled the Germans to rapidly abandon the town. Consequently, Cracow was one of the few Polish cities to be spared serious damages to its architecture. The great number of historical buildings renders it impossible to enumerate even those of highest value. The post-World War II Cracow has retained its status of a prominent educational, cultural and tourist centre. It has also become extensively industrialised. (I. J. K.)

The most ancient vestiges of architecture on Wawel Hill probably originate from the times of King Bolesław the Brave (turn of the 10th century), and include the best preserved Romanesque rotunda of St. Felix and St. Adauctus. The first Wawel Cathedral, constructed a century later in a fully evolved Romanesque style, contains the crypt of St. Leonard and a fragment of a tower. The existing Wawel complex has retained its originally Gothic plan. The ground-floor castle chambers, fortifications and three-nave main body of the cathedral are typical for 14th- and 15th-century forms. In time, they were dominated by the Renaissance style introduced at the time of the reconstruction of Wawel Castle (1502-1536) after a fire during the reign of Zygmunt the Old. The expansion of the royal residence was initiated by Francesco of Florence, brought over from Italy by the King from Hungary; the task, completed by Bartolomeo Berrecci, entailed the construction of three-storey courtyard galleries. The interior vaults are supported by thick, carved and painted beams, and the walls were embellished with frescoes or multi-hued tapestries, the most valuable being a group of 136 Arras hangings, commissioned in Brussels by Zygmunt Augustus (1550-1565). In 1517-1566, Berrecci constructed the Jagiellon mausoleum, adjoining the cathedral and known as the Zygmunt Chapel, the most splendid example of mature Renaissance architecture to be found beyond the Italian peninsula. Both the chapel and the royal sepulchres within served as models: numerous chapels-mausolea constructed by magnate and gentry families to the mid-17th century contained Italian-style sepulchres. The Zygmunt Chapel is crowned with an impressive marble cupola on an elevated drum pierced by round windows. The intrados is divided by means of caissons featuring rosettes of variegated design. Bas-relief mythological motifs, which in Renaissance Christianity symbolised the soul's way to salvation, adorn the interior walls. The naves and chapels of Wawel Cathedral — the coronation church of the Polish monarchs — contain Gothic royal tombs. The tomb of Władysław Jagiełło, presumably executed around 1430, during the king's lifetime, has a Renaissance canopy designed in 1519-1524 by Giovanni Cimni and Bartolomeo Berrecci, and

on the left:

Cracow. Wawel Hill, cathedral: the Zygmunt and Vasa chapels.

on pages 96-97:

■■ **Cracow.**
   The Floriańska Gate.

■■ **Cracow. Church of the Holy Virgin Mary.**

founded by Zygmunt the Old, the grandson of Władysław. The tomb of Kazimierz Jagiellon, a masterpiece from the end of the Middle Ages, was carved in marble by Wit Stwosz (Veit Stoss) of Nuremberg in about 1492 and placed in the Holy Cross chapel. The chapel walls were adorned with 15th-century Ruthenian-Byzantine polychrome, probably the most westerly example of this style. The Baroque sarcophagus of St. Stanisław, dating from 1669-1671, stands in the centre of the nave. The silver coffin, supported by angels and displaying scenes from the bishop's life, is the work of Peter van der Rennen, a Gdańsk artist of Flemish descent. The coffin, positioned under a canopy with a cupola, is an earlier design by the royal architect Giovanni Batista Travano, the most acclaimed artist working in Poland during the first half of the 17th century. The mediaeval town walls were demolished in the early 19th century, the only preserved fragments being the Floriańska Gate and the Barbakan (Barbican), erected at the end of the 15th century against the looming Turkish invasion. The Cracow Barbican is one of the rare examples of this type of construction in European architecture; originally, it was connected with the Floriańska Gate by a double line of defensive walls. (P. T.)

The church of the Holy Virgin Mary, popularly known as the "Mariacki church", was constructed in the 13th century in the Main Market Square for the Cracow burghers. The present-day edifice, dating from 1355-1365, is a three-nave Gothic basilica with a twin-tower façade. The loftier tower, from which the mediaeval *hejnał* (buglecall) is still sounded daily, possesses a highly original Late-Gothic cupola from 1478; that of the lower tower was completed in 1592 and is typical for the Renaissance style. The interior, featuring numerous works of art, received a polychrome decoration executed by Jan Matejko in 1889-1891. The Late Gothic pentaptych altar, carved in wood between 1477 and 1489 by Wit Stwosz, stands against the backdrop of the Gothic stained glass windows and occupies the entire presbytery. The central section of the open altar is composed of a scene representing the Assumption and on the

crowning of the altar, amidst the delicate forms of the canopy, he executed the Coronation. The altar rests on a predella portraying the Madonna's genealogical tree. Bas-reliefs on the side wings feature scenes spanning from the Annunciation to the Descent of the Holy Ghost. The closed wings of the altar show twelve scenes from the life of Christ and the Virgin Mary. During the Nazi occupation, the Germans removed the altar to Nuremberg; returned in 1946, it was subjected to careful conservation. Another work by Wit Stwosz featured in the church is a stone crucifix of harmonious beauty. (P. T.)

In 1364, Kazimierz the Great founded Cracow University, the most ancient academy in Central Europe after the university of Prague. Cracow became one of the most important European centres of intellectual life of the period. The oldest university building, Collegium Maius, was constructed in the 15th century by merging several older houses into a quadrilateral. The 15th century proved to be a golden era for the university; the intellectual current of the emergent Renaissance favoured learning, which in Cracow was additionally supported by printing techniques, rapidly developing from the 1470s. Cracow's reputation for achievements in the natural sciences, especially astronomy, as well as law (primarily international law), theology and ethics, attracted students from all parts of Central Europe. The university courtyard from the turn of the 15th century, with its characteristic stellar gallery vaulting, has been embellished with sculptures and fragments of the original Academy buildings. The first floor is composed of a series of reading rooms featuring painted decorations. According to legend, Dr. Faust, immortalised by Goethe's drama, studied in Cracow; unquestionable alumni include Nicholas Copernicus, Jan of Głogów, Marcin Bylica and other renowned scholars. The priceless collections of the University Museum were inaugurated by Marcin Bylica's astronomical instruments, donated to the university in 1491. (P. T)

Cracow. Collegium Maius, architectural details.

on the left:

Cracow. Collegium Maius, courtyard.

In 1079-1098, Palatine Sieciech, a highly influential dignitary in the duchy of Władysław Herman, founded the church of St. Andrew near his residential seat in the suburb of Okół. This unique example of Polish Romanesque art represents all the main elements of a monumental basilica designed on a smaller scale: three naves and a transept, but only a single bay. Two high towers with two-partite windows dominate the western façade, endowing the stone edifice, with its carefully arranged walls, with refined lightness. During the 14th century, Kazimierz the Great founded the autonomous town of Kazimierz outside the town walls of Cracow. The original population totalled 3 000 inhabitants, the vast majority of whom were Jews. At the end of the 15th century, King Jan Olbracht transferred the rest of Cracow's Jewish community to Kazimierz, which was incorporated into the main city in 1791. Despite the destruction caused during the second world war and the extermination of most of its inhabitants, Kazimierz has preserved many relics of Poland's Jewish heritage, including the Remuh cemetery and a number of synagogues, of which the oldest comes from the turn of the 14th century and was rebuilt by Santi Gucci at the end of the 16th century. Today, the Old Synagogue houses the Museum of Jewish History, Culture and Martyrdom, while the district of Kazimierz plays host to annual festivals of Jewish culture.

Cracow.
Baroque church
of St. Peter and Paul.

on the left:
Cracow.
Church of St. Andrew.

Cracow. "Manggha" – Centre of Japanese Art and Technology.

on the right:

Wiślica. Portal of the collegiate church of the Holy Virgin Mary with a foundation plaque.

The interiors of the church of St. Anne constitute one of the most valuable examples of Baroque art in Poland. The building was erected in 1689-1704 according to a design by Tylman van Gameren, a Dutch artist from Utrecht and the most accomplished architect working in Poland in the second half of the 17th century. The façade refers to the picturesque, chiaroscuro forms of the Roman Baroque. The architect took into consideration the necessity of viewing the abbreviaed form of the church in a narrow street, and introduced certain deformations. The acclaimed artists who designed the interiors included the Italian Baldassare Fontana, who executed the superb stuccoes; the frescoes are by Carlo and Innocenti Monti and Karol Dankwart, and the authors of the altar paintings are two renowned Polish Baroque artists: Jerzy Siemiginowski and Szymon Czechowicz. The exceptionally uniform interior represents an Italian Baroque attempt at attaining a stunning synthesis of the arts. (P. T.)

Cracow possesses up to a score of museums preserving testimony of the millennium of Polish history and displaying the largest art collections in Poland. Branches of the National Museum feature the richest collection of Polish art from the Middle Ages to modern times, works of the European masters, including Leonardo da Vinci and Rembrandt, and valuable arms and armour. The "Manggha" Centre of Japanese Art and Technology, opened in 1994 as another department of the National Museum, occupies a modern building with characteristic undulating lines, designed by the Japanese architect Arat Isozaki and situated on the bank of the Vistula opposite Wawel Hill. The basic core of the collection is composed of the exhibits amassed by Feliks Jasieński, who donated them to the National Museum in Cracow in 1920.

The chapel-mausoleum of the Firlej family in the parish church of the small town of Bejsce on the Nidzica, to the north-east of Cracow, was built in

1593-1601. This outstanding example of Polish Mannerism displays lavish carved decoration. After his voyage to Italy in 1569 Mikołaj Firlej, brought up as a Calvinist, became a fervent Catholic. The tombstone portrays him kneeling below a crucifix in accordance with the spirit of post-Tridentine devotion. The carefully educated Mikołaj was a prominent statesman of the post-Jagiellonian period and probably the first Polish archaeologist to conduct excavations.

Another interesting locality in the region is Wiślica, where King Kazimierz the Great announced his famous statutes. This monarch, commonly known to have "inherited a wooden Poland and left it built in stone", was the founder of many castles and churches, including the collegiate church in Wiślica. The Gothic edifice of slender proportions, erected in the third quarter of the 14th century, consists of a two-nave hall with an elongated presbytery and exquisitely traced, tripartite ribbed vaulting. The Ruthenian-Byzantine polychrome walls reflect the tastes of King Władysław Jagiełło, a subsequent patron of the church. Postwar investigations conducted under the church floor uncovered the crypt of an earlier Romanesque object. Its beautifully engraved floor - one of the most interesting examples of Romanesque art in Europe - displays symbolic creatures, the tree of life protected by lions, and figures associated with Duke Henryk of Sandomierz, the early 12th-century ruler of these lands, and his family. The Latin inscription expresses humility and hope for eternal salvation. (P. T.)

The fertile and picturesque Miechów Upland, considered one of the earliest areas of settlement in Poland, stretches to the north-east of Cracow, as far as the Nida Basin. Pińczów on the Nida, a food processing and quarry centre (marble), offers excellent tourism-recreation conditions (an artificial lake, interesting surroundings, hiking trails). In the 11th and 12th centuries, vineyards were cultivated in the vicinity of the castle-town. In 1429, the town received municipal status from Bishop Zbigniew Oleśnicki, who constructed a castle, a collegiate

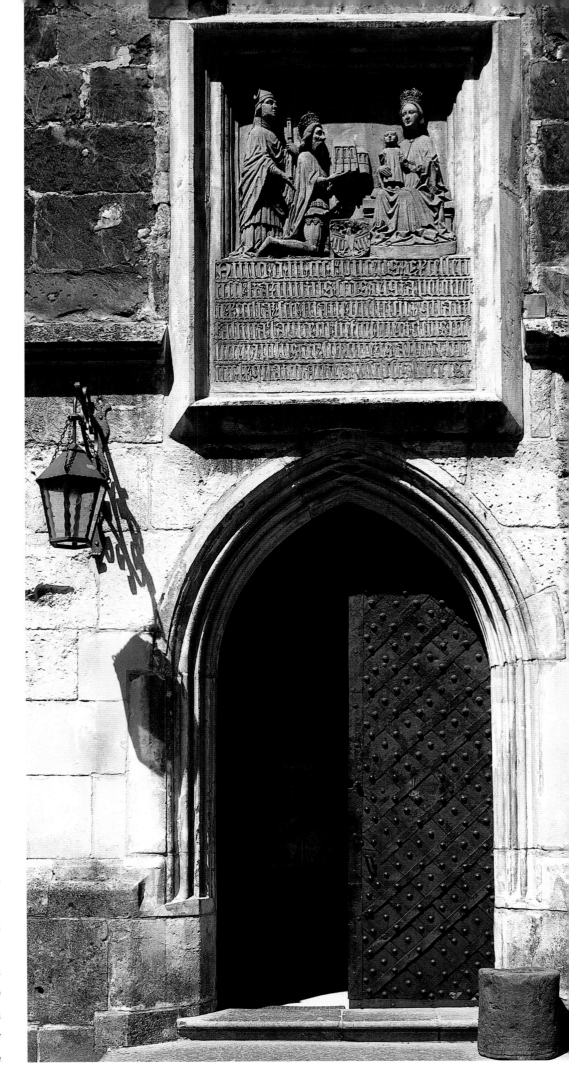

church, and a Paulite monastery. During the 16th century, Pińczów was one of the prime centres of the Polish Reformation movement; by the middle of the century, it became the main seat of the Polish Brethren, also known as the Arian Brothers, a radical offshoot of the Polish Calvinists, who created an important cultural and intellectual centre – the "Sarmatian Athens". After the banishment of the Polish Brethren the town declined. It was almost completely destroyed in September 1939, but postwar reconstruction retained the historic urban layout.

The village of Michałów, on the road to Działoszyce along the Mierzawa (a tributary of the Nida), is known for stud farms breeding Arab and tarpan horses as well as Shetland ponies. (I. J. K.)

The Chęciny chain, forming the southern fringe of the Świętokrzyskie Mts., is marked from a distance by the ruins of Chęciny Castle, built in 1296-1306. This was one of the most important defensive strongholds in Poland and a gathering place for the local nobility attending assemblies. Severely damaged during the Swedish wars, it fell into ruin. During the 15th-18th century, the townlet of Chęciny, lying at the foot of the castle, was an important lead and copper mining centre and

**Michałów.
Horses from a local
stud farm.**

on the left:

**Chęciny.
Ruins of castle.**

became known for stone-quarrying. A small but quite spectacular grotto known as "Raj" (Paradise), discovered in the vicinity, attracts numerous tourists. In it, archaeologists identified a site dating from the Middle Palaeolithic Age, with traces of flint tool production and animal remnants. (I. J. K.)

The chief town of the Świętokrzyskie Mts. region is Kielce, located in a picturesque basin. The town grew from a trading settlement, already mentioned in 11th-century documents. At the turn of the 11th century, it became the property of the bishops of Cracow and an administrative centre of their vast landed estates. In 1364, Kielce was granted municipal rights on the basis of Magdeburg law. Dynamic advancement in the 15th-17th century was the outcome of the development of the mining and processing of lead, copper and iron ore in nearby localities. This was the period of the origin of the splendid Early Baroque bishops' palace, constructed in 1637-1641 and today the seat of the National Museum. The interior contains preserved polychrome, magnificent plafonds from the T. Dolabella workshop, paintings, portals and mantelpieces. The adjacent cathedral was redesigned in 1632-1635 to become an Early Baroque basilica. In 1789, Kielce became the property of the Commonwealth. From 1816, it was a voivodeship capital; its subsequent status was that of a seat of a Russian gubernia and, finally, of a county. In 1816, Stanisław Staszic opened the Mining Academy and expanded the existing Mining Board so that it could reflect the growing mining and metallurgical industry in the Świętokrzyskie Mts. region (the Old Polish Basin). The decline of industry in the mid-19th century as well as the transference of the administrative centre to Radom seriously undermined the town's progress. Recovery came when a railway line was opened at the end of the 19th century, connecting Kielce with Dąbrowa Górnicza, Częstochowa and Warsaw. The rank of a voivodeship centre was restored once Poland regained independence in 1918. After the second world war, the town expanded thanks to an intensive growth of local industry. Kielce remains an interest-

ing city, and its location in the heart of the Świętokrzyskie Mts. draws visitors. The local folk costumes worn during holidays and for important family occasions frequently attract the attention of visitors. The costly attire has been handed over from generation to generation, and importance is attached not to the mere possession of the costume but to the manner of wearing it.

The Świętokrzyskie Mts. are the only in the whole Małopolska (Little Poland) Upland to rise significantly above sea level (despite slight altitudes) and to be arranged in ridges. The mountains consist of characteristic steep slopes with quartz rubble known as *gołoborze*, inselbergs and deeply incised valleys. After the Sudety Mts., these are the oldest mountains in Poland, with a well-preserved fold structure, composed of more than a dozen parallel subsidiary chains. The core is made up of the Łysogóry and

Świętokrzyskie Mts. Monastery on Mt. Święty Krzyż.

on the left:
Świętokrzyskie Mts. Slopes with quartz rubble.

on pages 108-109:
Kielce. Palace of the bishops of Cracow.

Krzemionki near Ostrowiec Świętokrzyski. The Krzemionki Archaeological Reservation.

on the right:

Świętokrzyskie Mts. Samsonów, ruins of an old iron foundry.

Dymińskie chains. The unique climate of the Świętokrzyskie range, and particularly the Łysogóry chain, is reflected in lower average temperatures, more abundant rainfall, and a shorter growing season. The mountain chains are covered with thick fir, larch and beech forests. Ancient vegetation has survived in Ice Age peatbogs; pine woods grow on the lower mountain levels, gradually giving way to mixed forests. The Łysogóry chain and certain adjoining areas constitute the Świętokrzyski National Park, composed of woodland, peatbogs, and geological and landscape reserves. Loess uplands stretch along a considerable part of the foothills, especially in the east. The highest peaks are found in the Łysogóry chain: Mt. Łysica (612 m), also known as Mt. St. Katarzyna (Catherine), with twin pinnacles and a large boulderfield, and Mt. Łysa Góra (595 m),

also named Mt. Święty Krzyż (Holy Cross) or Łysiec, with the most extensive scree. In prehistoric times, Mt. Łysa Góra was the site of a pagan cult, evidenced by a stone mound (1, 2 km long) encircling the peak and legends about witches' sabbaths. A Benedictine abbey built here in 1103 remained active until the cassation of the order in 1818. The abbey complex consists of quadrilateraly arranged buildings (14th-15th century) with a cloister and a Gothic gallery, the Early Baroque Oleśnicki chapel (17th century), and a Baroque-Classical church (18th century). The monastery is surrounded by the dense, tenebrous Jodłowa (Fir) Forest. (I. J. K.).

The Świętokrzyskie Mts. and the surrounding countryside were the cradle of Polish mining and metallurgy. The celebrated archaeological reservation of Krzemionki Opatowskie includes a Neolithic flint mine, with more than 700 vertical shafts linked by means of galleries, a ventilation system, props and intentionally preserved pillars. The tools produced here were exported to destinations hundreds of kilometres away. Copper, iron and lead ores were mined already two thousand years ago. In Roman times (second and third century A. D.), this was one of the largest iron mining and metallurgy centres in Europe, producing tools, weapons and nails. Metallurgy based on blast furnaces prospered in the 15th and 16th century, using water power supplied by local rivers and wood for firing the furnaces. In 1598, the first smelting furnace burning charcoal introduced at Samsonów proved more productive than its predecessors, but furnaces of this sort were not universal until the 18th century. Forges used by blacksmiths, tinsmith workshops and workshops making axes and pipes grew up around the foundries. The 1820s and 1830s were the last period conducive for the Old Polish Basin; it was then that the autonomous government of the Kingdom of Poland embarked upon planned industrialisation, and invested considerable funds into the expansion of the iron industry on the banks of the Kamienna, Bobrza and Czarna rivers. Works established upstream supplied those operating further down the

rivers with raw materials and semi-finished products. After the November Uprising, the local industry continued to be financially supported by the Bank of Poland (until 1845). Many examples of old industrial buildings have survived from this period, including the ruins of a blast furnace in Samsonów, a dam in Nietulisko, a puddling furnace and a rolling mill, a Classicist administrative building, and a workers' housing estate in Sielpia Wielka. The majority of the enterprises went bankrupt in the second half of the 19th century when charcoal-burning foundries became obsolete owing to the introduction of coal. Ostrowiec and Starachowice, connected by railway with the Dąbrowa Górnicza coal basin, were the only two centres which continued operating.

The Old Polish Industrial District has become an additional tourist attraction of the Świętokrzyskie Mts. Sightseers also admire the beautiful countryside and its unique landmarks, such as the "Bartek" oak near Samsonów, one of the most ancient trees in Poland, estimated to be more than 1 000 years old. The circumference of the trunk, unfortunately gravely damaged by lightning, totals 13.4 m.

Szydłowiec lies on the north eastern edge of the Świętokrzyskie Mts., within the range of the voivodeship of Mazovia. This former centre of magnate landed estates has served sandstone quarrying and tooling since the Middle Ages. Extant historic monuments include the castle of the Szydłowiecki family (16th century, rebuilt in the following century by the Radziwiłłs), a parish church from the turn of the 14th century, and a Late Renaissance town hall erected in 1602-1626. A Jewish cemetery with tombstones from the 18th and 19th centuries is an uncommon vestige of the past. The Museum of Folk Musical Instruments (in the castle) is also worth a visit. (I.J.K)

To the north, the Kielce Upland is preceded by the Iłża Foothills. The first traces of settlement in the environs of Iłża originate from the Late Neolithic Age (about the 10th millennium B. C.) and are composed of a workshop with numerous flint tools. During the Early Middle Ages, the settlement assumed the form

on the left:

**Ujazd. Ruins of
Krzyżtopór Castle.**

of a wooden defensive castle-town, which received municipal rights in the first half of the 13th century. The extant ruins of the mediaeval castle of the bishops of Cracow, mentioned by Jan Długosz, include the round tower on Castle Hill, which offers a superb view of the surrounding countryside.

In 1627-1644, the Italian architect Lorenzo Senes constructed a castle called Krzyżtopór for Krzysztof Ossoliński near the present-day village of Ujazd. An exceptional artistic programme, immense scale and astonishing spatial solutions render this Mannerist residence one of the most individualistic architectural monuments in Europe. Plundered and burned by the Swedes in 1655, the castle functioned for barely eleven years, a manifestation of Sarmatian pride and predilection for opulence. Inscribed into a regular five-sided arrangement of bastions and encircled with a moat, it symbolised the continuity of the Ossoliński family; the number of the towers, hall, chambers and windows corresponded to the seasons, months, weeks, and days in the year. The façade was embellished by colourful sgrafitto with the signs of the Zodiac and a genealogical tree reaching back, in accordance with Sarmatian ideology, to ancient Rome. The palace complex was traversed by a small road leading to an elliptical courtyard with a four-storeyed arcade, a passage to sumptuous chambers ten metres high and with seven-meter high windows. One of the bastions contained a drawing room with an astounding aquarium full of tropical fish in the place of a ceiling. The castle, which took its name from the coat of arms displayed above the entrance gate – a cross (*krzyż*) and an axe (*topór*) – is probably the most perfect combination of Western Mannerism and Polish Sarmatian ideology.

In 1643-1650, the same architect designed a second unusual building, this time for Jerzy Ossoliński: the collegiate church in Klimontów. The elliptical nave is surrounded on the inside by two-storeyed vaulted galleries; passages hewn in the thick walls make it possible to circumvent the church at each level. As in Krzyżtopór, the architect demonstrated virtuosity devoid of all functional justification by creating a work of art for art's sake, in a spirit typical of Man-

on pages 118-119:

Szydłowiec. Castle.

Sandomierz.

Castle.

on the right:

Sandomierz.

Town hall.

nerism. The town walls, castle and church at Szydłów date back to the days of Kazimierz the Great and constitute a well-preserved complex of Gothic architecture from the mid-14th century. (P. T.)

Sandomierz, one of the most beautiful towns in Poland, lies on the Vistula, on the steep edge of the Sandomierz Upland crisscrossed by loess ravines. Its origins go back to an 8th-9th century tribal centre, which during the reign of Bolesław the Brave became an important ducal residence and castle-town. At the time of the country's feudal fragmentation, Sandomierz was the capital of a sovereign duchy and, subsequently, the seat of a voivodeship. Situated at the crossroads of routes from Hungary

and Rus', the town was frequently raided by Ruthenians, Lithuanians and Tartars. At the beginning of the 13th century, Duke Leszek the White built a castle, and in 1286 Leszek the Black granted the city municipal status, based on Magdeburg law, together with numerous trading privileges. Kazimierz the Great enclosed the borough with a defence wall and remodelled the castle as well as the small town hall. In the 15th-16th century, Sadomierz owed its prosperity to a growing trade in grain shipped down the Vistula to Gdańsk. The burghers also profited from trade in Carpathian timber, constructed a river shipyard, and supported the development of the crafts. The increasingly wealthy town expanded – this was the period of the origin of its

most splendid buildings and the municipal water supply system (mid-16th century). Sandomierz also flourished as a cultural centre: its inhabitants included outstanding humanists and Renaissance artists. Decline came as an aftermath of 17th- and 18th-century wars, and during the partitions Sandomierz was reduced to a small frontier townlet. Its economic position revived during the inter-war period, especially the late 1930s, when it became part of the Central Industrial District.

Picturesque location and one of the most valuable complexes of historic monuments of architecture in Poland enabled Sandomierz to become an important tourist centre. The oldest extant building is the Late Romanesque brick church of St. James, part of a Dominican monastery complex from 1226.

The present-day cathedral, founded as a collegiate church in 1360, contains well-preserved Ruthenian-Byzantine frescoes from the first half of the 15th century. The so-called house of Jan Długosz, a Gothic mansion, also comes from that century. Only the west wing with Gothic towers has remained of the castle. The large Market Square, surrounded by old town houses, contains a fine town hall, built in the mid-14th century and in the 16th century remodelled in the Renaissance style. The Vistula escarpment features a wing of the so-called Gostomianum, a Renaissance Jesuit collegiate church, founded in 1605-1615, which housed the oldest grammar school for young nobles in Poland. The entire Old Town quarter, surrounded by a partly preserved town wall with the 14th-century Opatowska Gate, constitutes a unique complex of Romanesque, Gothic and Renaissance town planning, whose architecture ranges from Romanesque to Baroque.

The numerous loess ravines in the countryside around Sandomierz include the Queen Jadwiga ravine, more than 400 m long and cutting deeply into the undersoil. (I. J. K.)

The Cistercian order played an important part in the evolution of Polish architecture in the first half of the 13th century. Stone monasteries and churches displayed the excellent construction of cross-ribbed

vaulting, for the first time based on the ogee arch as well as sophisticated albeit spare decoration concentrated on column capitals. All Cistercian complexes followed a similar plan and spatial design. Abbeys in Wąchock, Koprzywnica and Sulejów emulated Fontenay Abbey in France, and consist of a three-nave basilica with a transept, a towerless façade, and a monastery complex adjacent to the south and constructed around a square courtyard. Cistercian architecture was a breakthrough in building technique and paved the way towards the abetment of Gothic construction, which in Poland appeared in the middle of the 13th century. (P. T.)

The Land of Staszów, along the so-called Cistercian Route, includes the noteworthy town of Kurozwęki with a refurbished Baroque-Classicist palace, recent-

**Wąchock.
Cistercian abbey,
chapter house.**

on the left:

**Wąchock.
Cistercian abbey,
view from the west.**

ly restored to its owner and displaying a characteristic Pompean rose façade. The locality has been known for the local stud breeding Arab horses, additionally renowned for Kasztanka, the favourite mare of Marshal Józef Piłsudski. From autumn 2000, Kurozwęki became celebrated for breeding American bisons, the first such venture in Poland.

The rolling plain of the Lublin Upland is covered with a network of river valleys with gentle slopes, crisscrossed by ravines. The fertile soils encouraged the development of the now dominant agriculture. Industry, primarily connected with food processing, has been developed only recently. The town of Kazimierz Dolny, on the western border of the Lublin Upland, in the river-gate Vistula valley, boasts of unique architecture and landscape. This small centre serving the neighbouring farming region is simulta-

neously an important tourist destination and one of the most popular vacation spots in Poland. The town buildings are concentrated around the Market Square at a point where the Vistula forms steep escarpments. Houses nestling amidst orchards line the streets which branch off from the Square to fill the whole breadth of the valley, all the way to the water's edge. The towers of old churches soar above the town houses; higher still perch the picturesque ruins of a royal castle with a tower. It is not surprising that every step of the way one may encounter painters at their easels, and that visitors include representatives of the world of the arts, literature and science, seeking both inspiration and repose.

The name of the town is generally associated with King Kazimierz the Great, although the history of the settlement goes back to more ancient days. From an 11th-century village belonging to the Premon-

**Kazimierz Dolny.
View of the parish
church seen from the
market square.**

on the left:

**Sandomierz Upland.
The Queen Jadwiga
ravine.**

**Kazimierz Dolny.
Granary.**

on the right:

**Kazimierz Dolny.
The Przybyła town
houses: "St. Nicholas"
and "St. Christopher".**

on pages 128-129:

Janowiec. Castle

stratensian nuns of Zwierzyniec near Cracow, Kazimierz became a parish seat (1315). Already at the
time, it bore the present-day name suggesting that it
owed its foundation to Kazimierz the Just (end of
12th century). Municipal rights were, however,
granted in the mid-14th century by Kazimierz the
Great, who also built a fortified castle, a fact con-
firmed by Jan Długosz. During the 16th century, the
castle was rebuilt by the Firlej family, and by 1774 it
was abandoned. Recent restoration consisted of protecting and elevating part of the castle walls. The
fortuitous position of Kazimierz favoured its growth.
A ford was created across the Vistula on a trade
route from Lvov to Silesia and Greater Poland. Traffic along this trail, busy already during the mid-14th
century, became particularly lively in the 16th century. At the time, Kazimierz was crossed by yet
another trade route – between Rus' and Prussia. The
town flourished thanks to the development of grain
production in the Lublin region and the growing Vistula grain trade. Barges carrying grain from the

on the right:

Lublin. Castle

Lublin Upland sailed down the Vistula to Gdańsk, and Kazimierz became an important river port and grain shipment centre. During the last quarter of the 16th century, the town was responsible for 16% of the Vistula grain trade. Several score granaries were constructed for storage purposes. The grain trade yielded impressive merchant fortunes, evidenced by the extant, richly ornamented Manneristic town residence of Michał and Krzysztof Przybyła and the house known as "Celejowska". Wars raging in the mid-17th century put an end to the period of prosperity. Revival in the late 19th century was the outcome of the growing influx of tourists, which continued to grow in inter-war Poland and rendered Kazimierz a popular summer resort. Ravaged in the second world war, the town was rapidly rebuilt. Historical buildings were meticulously repaired and partially restored, while new ones match the unique local architecture. Vacation homes, boarding houses and hostels have been constructed to accommodate the increasing numbers of visitors. (I. J. K.)

Lublin, situated amid gently rolling loess hills on the River Bystrzyca, a tributary of the Wieprz, has been the main centre of the Lublin Upland since the 12th century. The town grew from a stronghold on the Polish-Ruthenian border. Destroyed by numerous Ruthenian and Lithuanian invasions, it was granted municipal rights upon the basis of document issued in 1317 by Kazimierz the Great, who built a castle, encircled the town with defence walls, and granted numerous privileges. Trade with Lithuania and Rus' thrived, and local fairs attracted merchants from different countries. Lublin also became a prominent cultural and political centre. Polish-Lithuanian councils, conventions and Diet assemblies were held here; in 1569, the town witnessed the signing of a union between Poland and Lithuania. The Crown Tribunal – the supreme court of the gentry from Little Poland – was established in Lublin in 1578. The Cossack and Swedish wars, plagues and fires contributed to the town's descent. In the 19th century, Lublin became the seat of a gubernia, and local industry grew after the construction of a railway line

major economic, academic and cultural centre in south-eastern Poland. Those of its numerous historical monuments which were damaged during the war have been carefully restored, particularly in the Old Town, a task which required almost ten years. The most valuable monuments include the town hall, repeatedly redesigned, the last time in 1781 in the Classical style, Renaissance and Baroque town houses, sections of the old defence walls with three gates, and the Dominican monastic complex from 1342, which today is a Renaissance edifice with Baroque towers and a fragment of the original Gothic building. The cathedral, a former Jesuit collegiate church from the turn of the 16th century, features a Classicist portico designed by Antonio Corazzi in 1819. Several monastery complexes constructed in the 15th and 17th century are located outside the Old Town. The castle, remodelled during the 19th century in the Neo-Gothic style, with a preserved old tower and the Gothic chapel of the Holy Trinity (second half of the 14th century), featuring Ruthenian-Byzantine polychrome, rises on a hill above the Old Town.

In 1941, the Nazis set up a death camp at Majdanek, a suburb of Lublin, which claimed the lives of 360 000 persons of 51 nationalities (the majority of the inmates was composedof Jews and Poles).

A monument unveiled in 1969 commemorates the victims (I. J. K.)

Lublin.
Majdanek, Nazi
concentration camp.

on the right:
Lublin.
The Krakowska Gate.

(1877). The first post-partition Polish government was set up here on 7 November 1918. New factories and cultural institutions were opened during the inter-war years. The second world war signified extensive devastation and heavy loss of life. From its liberation in July 1944 to the time when Warsaw was freed in January 1945 Lublin fulfilled the function of the capital of Poland. The first higher school to be opened in postwar Poland was the Maria Skłodowska-Curie University of Lublin. Postwar Lublin developed rapidly, predominantly owing to local industry. The town expanded and encompassed new residential and industrial districts. At present, Lublin is the

The town of Chełm is located in Volhynian Polesie, along the eastern edge of the Lublin Upland. This former tribal stronghold of the Lendzianie received municipal rights in 1392. The interior of the important post-Piarist church is an excellent example of the Late Baroque style from the mid-18th century, when Rome and her architectural monuments had ceased to serve as a model. The architects of Austria, southern Germany and Bohemia proposed new, complicated spatial arrangements, skillfully combining longitudinal and central plans. In Poland, Paolo Fontana, an architect from the Italian-Swiss borderland, designed a number of buildings maintained in this spirit. The nave in Chełm is based on a ground

plan close to an ellipse, with vaulting embellished with illusionistic polychrome (1758). The interior decoration is primarily Rococo. Zamość, a town mentioned on the UNESCO world cultural heritage list, lies in the south-eastern part of the voivodeship of Lublin. Founded in 1558, it rapidly developed as a trade and crafts centre. The Zamość Academy was opened in 1595. In 1579, the Venetian, Bernardo Morando drew up plans of a new town for the royal Chancellor Jan Zamoyski, a renowned statesman educated at the universities of Paris, Rome and Padua. A considerable fragment of the project, based on Italian theoretical regular plans, has survived. Zamość was encircled by defence walls with bastions and a moat. In 1639-1651, a centrally placed town hall was added; its elevation features a commanding

enscarped tower, with fragmented, delicate architectural detail. The resulting effects of contrast and lack of cohesion are typical of Mannerism, which also defined the style of the collegiate church from 1587-1600. In contrast to Renaissance churches the interior is based on contrasts between a lofty main nave and a low, elongated presbytery, as well as on vivid chiaroscuro. The geometrically arranged stucco lintels decorating the vaulting are typical of early–17th century Polish Mannerism. Although modelled on Italian forms, the architecture of Zamość, constructed until the mid–17th century, had increasingly little in common with the Italian Renaissance, just as Zamoyski, a propagator of the Counter-Reformation, was no longer an exemplary Renaissance humanist. (P. T.)

Zamość.
Renaissance houses
in the market square.

on the left:
Zamość. Town hall.

The Sudety Mts. and The Silesian Lowland

T he Karkonosze Mts. comprise the highest massif of the Sudety Mts. The altitude of the main ridge, built mainly of granite, ranges from 1 300 to 1 400 m; very few peaks rise above this level, including the highest summit – Mt. Snieżka (1 602 m), covered with scree and the site of a meteorological station and a tourist shelter. Mt. Śnieżka offers a view of the whole Sudety Mts., and on a clear night the lights of Prague, some 80 km to the south-east, are visible. The climate is severe, and snow covers Mt. Śnieżka an average of 194 days annually. A specific feature of the Karkonosze Mts. are the numerous scattered groups of rocks, assuming fantastic shapes, such as Pielgrzymy (the Pilgrims). Post-glacial hollows, containing mountain lakes, feature relic plants. Lake Mały lies in such a basin, surrounded by the steep, 200 m-high slopes of Mt. Śnieżka.

K arpacz, located below Mt. Śnieżka, was founded in the 14th century as a settlement for speculators in gold and semi-precious stones. In the 17th century, it became known for herb collectors and producers of medicines. Since the mid-19th century, Karpacz remains a growing tourist and leisure centre, specialising in winter sports. It is one of the largest resorts in the Sudety Mts. and a chief base for excursions into the eastern Karkonosze. A special attraction for the visitors is the so-called Vang temple, a richly carved wooden church from the first half of the 13th century, shipped in the 19th century from the small town of Vang (southern Norway) and partially reconstructed and redesigned in Karpacz. (I. J. K.)

on the right:

Landscape in the region of Mt. Ślęża.

The main urban centre in the Jelenia Góra Basin is the town of Jelenia Góra, originally a defensive settlement. In 1108-1111, King Bolesław the Wry-mouth built a fortified castle on the left bank of the River Kamienna. Jelenia Góra received municipal rights most probably in the middle or at the end of the 13th century, when it had already become a large trading centre. Iron mining, smelting and processing developed in the vicinity of the borough. The 14th and 15th century witnessed the growth of the role played by the urban crafts and the increasing significance of glass production and, subsequently, weaving, which enjoyed a leading position in the town's flourishing economic life from the 16th to the 18th century. Jelenia Góra produced the finest fab-

rics, such as batiste and voile, not made anywhere else in Silesia. Cloth fairs held from the end of the 16th century were the largest in the region; the local products attracted buyers from all the important European markets, and from the 17th century were shipped also to Africa and America. Polished crystal glassware evolved out of late mediaeval glass production. Economic development was curtailed after the town's incorporation into Prussia in 1740, and the beginning of the 19th century signified a decline of the weaving trade. The revival of economic life in the second half of the 19th century was associated with the advancement of textile mills and the rise of the ceramic and paper industry. In postwar Poland, the town, only slightly affected by the second world

Jelenia Góra.
Market Square.

on the left:

Karpacz.
The Wang temple.

ornamental fountain with a statue of Neptune. Jelenia Góra was an important Reformation centre: a Protestant school, famous for its high academic level, was founded during the 16th century; at the time of the Counter-Reformation it was appropriated by the Jesuits. The Evangelical church of Divine Grace (1709-1718), with galleries and loggias for 400 people and an organ mounted above the main altar, testifies to the town's support for Protestant traditions. The church was erected after the Catholic Emperor of Austria expressed his consent under pressure from the King of Sweden, and was designed by the Swedish architect Frantz of Reval (today: Tallin), who drew inspiration from St. Catherine's in Stockholm. The municipal Dramatic Theatre is an important cultural institution responsible for international street theatre meetings, which enliven also the cultural life of nearby localities. (L. J. K.)

Lwówek Śląski, one of Silesia's oldest towns, lies on the River Bóbr, along the borderline between the Kaczawskie and Izerskie Foothills. The town, which owed its earliest development to nearby beds of gold and silver, was granted municipal status in 1217 by Duke Henry the Bearded. Situated on a trade route leading from Germany to Rus', Lwówek began to prosper in earnest during the 16th and early 17th century thanks to the local crafts, particularly linen and cloth manufacturing. Almost completely destroyed during the Thirty Years War, it never regained its former prominence despite the fact that during the 18th century it remained an important linen production centre. Ravaged in the course of the second world war, Lwówek preserved a number of historical monuments, including the noteworthy 14th-century Gothic-Renaissance town hall with an entrance hall featuring magnificent Late Gothic (socalled Władysław) vaulting, and Renaissance and Baroque houses erected in the Market Square during the 16th and 18th century.

Mt. Ostrzyca (499 m), the highest peak in the Kaczawskie Foothills, is a basalt, uniformly shaped vestige of an extinct volcano. The mountain slopes are covered with rich deciduous forests, and in parts with

Ślęża. Pagan cult sculpture.

on the right:

Strzegom. Portal of the church of St. Peter and Paul.

war, became an important administrative and educational centre, and concentrated assorted branches of industry. Today, Jelenia Góra acts as a base for tourists and holidaymakers visiting the western Sudety range. The spa of Cieplice Zdrój, since 1976 part of the municipality, and the historic Old Town enhance the attractiveness of the city. Numerous historical monuments reflect the splend our of bygone days. The charming Market Square, at the heart of the old mediaeval quarter, is surrounded by arcaded Baroque town houses from the 17th and 18th century. The centrally-placed 16th-century town hall, redesigned in the 17th century, faces an rocky debris. The characteristic vegetation and rock forms are under protection. To the east of the Kaczawskie Foothills lies Bolków, a 13th-century trading settlement, today an industrial, vacation and tourist centre on the River Nysa Szalona. The town, which has retained its mediaeval urban layout and historic character, nestles at the foot of a hillock, on top of which there stands a mighty castle built at the end of the 13th century by Bolko I, the Duke of Świdnik, after whom the town was named. The castle was connected with the town's defence walls. Expanded during the 14th and 16th century, besieged and captured upon many occasions, it partially fell into ruin. The northern, better preserved part of the castle now houses a department of the Regional Museum in Jelenia Góra. The main tower, standing in the castle courtyard, provides an excellent view of the town and countryside. The castle is surrounded by two rows of walls connecting it with the city. The elongated Market Square is situated on the axis of a former trade route from Jawor to Kamienna Góra. The northern row of houses in the Market Square is composed of attractive 16th-- and 17th-century arcaded edifices.

Mt. Ślęża (718 m), known also as Sobótka, is the highest peak of the Sudety Foothills. From the 8th to the 11th century it was the paramount site of the pagan cult of the Ślężanie, a Western Slavonic tribe from which the name of Silesia is derived. The mountain top was surrounded by stone mounds, the remains of which can be seen today together with five stone cult statues, linked with the Celtic civilisation. (I. J. K.)

During the 14th century, Silesia, subdivided into small principalities, became a fief of John of Luxembourg, the King of Bohemia. The attempts made by Kazimierz the Great to reunite the province with the Polish Kingdom came to naught. Only the duchy of Jawor-Świdnica retained its independence until the end of the century. This political situation introduced Silesian art to the impact of Prague and Vienna, conspicuously testified by the Gothic church of St. Peter and Paul at Strzegom (second half of the 14th century). The church, built by the Joannites, represents a

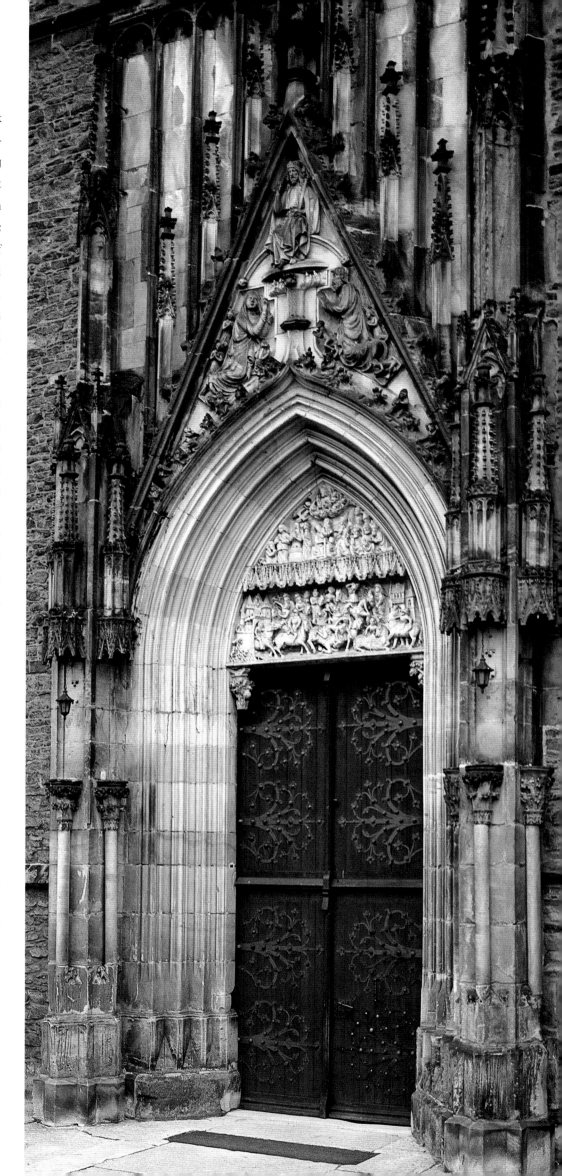

virtually complete plan for a great cathedral. The style of the richly sculpted portals refers to the Prague workshop of the Parler family. A depiction of the Last Judgment adorns the gable, while the tympanum illustrates the life and conversion of St. Paul, portrayed in dynamic scenes brimming with dramatic tension. The parish church in Świdnica on the Bystrzyca – a Gothic 14th-century basilica, remodelled in the 16th century on a central ground plan into a hall church, comes from the same period. The nave is closed by the original main altar. The circular construction, surmounted on seven columns and with a rich coping designed by Johann Riedel in 1690-1694, symbolises the Old Testament House of Wisdom or the Throne of Solomon. A greater part of the interior dates back to the 18th century, and is the work of Georg Leonard Weber, a local sculptor

and the author of figures of the saints decorating the church pillars, and the Heavenly Orchestra, which he used in 1704-1708 for embellishing the organ. In the wake of the Treaty of Westphalia, the Catholic authorities permitted the Protestants of Silesia to erect three churches on the condition that they were to be built outside towns and include impermanent half-timbered walls. One such church was raised in Świdnica in 1656; the ingenious wooden construction of the vast interior made it possible to accommodate 3 500 seated members of the congregation. The Late Baroque outfitting includes a magnificent pulpit and an altar with the scene of the *Baptism of Jesus Christ*. (P. T.)

The castle of Książ stands on a woody hillock in a spacious park in the suburbs of the industrial town

**Książ Castle
in Wałbrzych.**

on the left:

**Świdnica. Portal of
the Gothic church
of St. Stanisław and
Wacław.**

of Wałbrzych. The sprawling edifice is the result of centuries-long remodelling: from a late-13th century Gothic castle of the dukes of Świdnica through Renaissance and Baroque designs to complete refurbishing in the Neo-Renaissance spirit at the beginning of the 20th century. After World War II, the castle was devastated; lengthy conservation, initiated in 1966, reconstructed the Late Baroque ballroom from the first half of the 18th century. Today, part of the castle interiors is open to the public, and the rest has been turned into a hotel with conference and restaurant facilities. (P. T.)

The Thirty Years War was followed by a period of intense building, connected primarily with the Counter-Reformation in Silesia. New monastery complexes arose, existing churches received generous, Late Baroque decorations, and pilgrim centres were founded. This activity became particularly determined between 1690 and 1740. Silesian architects continued to emulate works by Fischer von Erlach, Hildebrandt and the Dientzenhofers of Vienna and Prague. Excellent but anonymous examples of such architecture include two churches in the village of Krzeszów, former monastic property whose history is closely connected with the local Cistercian abbey. The church of St. Joseph, built in 1690-1696, displays a wonderful polychrome by Michael Willmann. The other is a Late Baroque Cistercian church constructed in 1728-1735 on the site of its mediaeval predecessor. The picturesque twin-tower façade with elegant detail reveals an exceptional soaring

■ **Książ Castle: fireplace in the ballroom.**

■ **Krzeszów. Interior of a Cistercian church.**

on the left:

Książ Castle.

**Chełmsko Śląskie.
Weavers' houses.**

dynamic comparable only to the Gothic style, and contrasts with the relatively low church body and modest exterior. The interior, however, complements the façade – typically Late Baroque space was shaped by means of a suitable configuration of the concave-convex walls of the nave and chapel, as well as the broken and multiplied pilasters. The vaulting was decorated with a remarkable polychrome by Georg Wilhelm Neuhertz as well as stucco and sculptural details by Ferdinand Brokof and Antonio Dorasil. The Cistercian church in Krzeszów is a veritable master-piece of European Late Baroque art.

The church in Wambierzyce, a village at the foot of the Stołowe Mts., lacks the artistic qualities of the Krzeszów churches. A wide façade at the top of a monumental staircase serves as a backdrop for religious celebrations which attract pilgrims from all of Silesia. The circular, somewhat flat façade leads to a complex labyrinthian interior, and the extended octagonal main nave is covered with an elliptical dome. The edifice, which dates from 1715-1720, was the result of the enlargement of an earlier church.

on the right:

**Wambierzyce.
Pilgrims' church.**

The highly original historical monument in Chełmsko Śląskie – eleven weavers' houses (one has not survived), known as the Twelve Apostles – comes from the same period (early 18th century). The arcaded, wooden skeleton-construction houses are part of a larger complex, preserved only in part. (P. T.)

The holiday-tourist resort of Sokolec, which offers excellent skiing conditions, is a village situated below Mt. Wielka Sowa, the highest peak in the Sowie Mts., a range belonging to the Central Sudety and built from pre-Cambrian gneiss, the oldest in Silesia. The village of Zagórze Śląskie on the north-western edge of the Sowie Mts. is a favourite holiday spot for the inhabitants of such nearby towns as Wałbrzych and Świdnica, although summer visitors are beginning to come from further afield. The village owes its popularity to attractive location on the River Bystrzyca, a tributary of the Odra, near the artificial Lake Lubachowski, which lies in a valley among steeply sloping and heavily wooded hills. A well-equipped water sports centre verges on a tourist base for excursions into the nearby Sowie Mts. The picturesque, wooded Mt. Choina (450 m) near Zagórze Śląskie is partially incorporated into a landscape reservation; its peak is topped with the ruins of Grodno Castle, towering over Bystrzyca and its environs. This is one of the oldest monuments of architecture in Lower Silesia, built in the early 14th century by Duke Bolko I of Świdnica. Enlarged and redesigned in the 14th and 16th century, the castle retained Gothic and Renaissance fragments. Ravaged during the Thirty Years War, it fell into ruin and was partially rebuilt and reconstructed during the 19th century. Today, it houses a regional museum. The Stołowe Mts. are a characteristic group in the Central Sudety Mts.; built of Tertiary sandstone comprising two strata they are separated from each other and the surroundings by perpendicular rocks. The top layer consists of several isolated, cracked blocks; weathering has formed labyrinths and unusual rock formations. (I. J K.)

on the left:

Sowie Mts.

**Kłodzka Basin.
Międzygórze, the
Wilczka Waterfall.**

One of the most frequented recreation areas in Poland is the Kłodzko Basin, the largest intermontane hollow in the Sudety Mts., conspicuous for its picturesque landscape, mild climate, numerous mineral springs (acidulous and sulphur), and mud baths. Recreation and tourist centres, health resorts and spas abound; many of them were created in old settlements full of historical monuments, which act as an additional attraction. Duszniki has functioned as a spa since the turn of the 18th century, although its mineral springs were known already in 1408. The spa developed in an old industrial urban settlement whose inhabitants earned their living from extracting and smelting iron ore from the Middle Ages until 1879, and from weaving (since the 16th century). One of the oldest paper mills in Poland was opened

on the right:

Stołowe Mts.

**Kłodzka Basin.
Duszniki-Zdrój,
old paper-mill.**

on the right:
**Zagórze Śląskie.
Grodno Castle,
view from a tower.**

here in 1562. A wooden mill from 1605 is one of the many historic buildings in the town. Every August, the Frederick Chopin piano festival held in Duszniki commemorates the composer's visit in 1826. Międzygórze, situated in the deep wooded valley of the River Wilczka, is a pleasant holiday and health resort. The first settlement was founded in the 15th century by woodcutters and charcoal burners. The greatest local landmark is the largest waterfall in the Sudety Mts., the next attraction being boarding houses built in the Swiss and Norwegian style. (I. J. K.)

Bystrzyca Kłodzka, on the high bank of the Nysa Kłodzka and its confluence with the Bystrzyca, grew out of an 11th-century Slavic settlement. From the Middle Ages, the town was an important industrial centre, once specialising in textile production and today known for its wood-paper industry. Bystrzyca has preserved the appearance of a mediaeval fortified town as well as numerous historical monuments from assorted epochs, starting with the 13th century and including a Gothic church and town houses from the 17th century. Local highlights include a unique museum of match box labels.

Lądek Zdrój – a town founded in the 13th century and a spa with equally ancient traditions lies between the Złote Mts. and Mt. Śnieżnik. Mention of the healing properties of the local springs was first made in 1272, and bathing facilities were set up in the late 15th century. As in the case of other towns in the Kłodzko Basin, the spa developed during the 19th century; its celebrated patients included

**Lądek Zdrój.
Town hall.**

on the right:

Bystrzyca Kłodzka.

Johann Wolfgang Goethe and Ivan Turgenev. The historical monuments in Lądek encompass a valuable complex of Baroque-façade town houses from the 16th and 17th century in the Market Square, and an old arched stone bridge over the Biała Lądecka. The main urban centre in the Basin is Kłodzko, one of Silesia's oldest settlements, mentioned in documents from 981 as a stronghold on the Polish-Bohemian border; first reference to a "town" was made in 1114. Together with the entire Kłodzko region, the city changed hands back and forth between the Poles and the Bohemians, to become a fief of the Bohemian kings in 1348. Annexed, together with Bohemia, by Austria during the 16th century, Kłodzko was incorporated into Prussia in about the middle of the 18th century in the wake of a war of succession. The growth of the town, benefiting

from an important trade route, was halted, and Kłodzko started to fulfil predominantly strategic functions – until 1877 it was one of the main fortresses in Prussia. Despite the twists and turns of fate, Kłodzko for a long time retained lively contacts with Poland – it was the birthplace of the 14th-century *Floriański Psalter*, one of the oldest monuments of Polish literature. As late as the 18th century, all municipal documents were recorded in Polish. (I. J. K.)

Henryków, a settlement founded in 1225 by Duke Henry the Bearded next to a Cistercian monastery, another of his foundations, lies in the Sudety Foothills, in the central part of the Strzelińskie Hills, on the River Oława, a tributary of the Odra. Up to the mid-18th century, the monastery was the economic and cultural centre of this part of Silesia. The so-called *Księga Henrykowska* (The Henryków Book), written here in 1268-1273 (and continued during the 14th century), today kept in the Archdiocesan Archive in Wrocław, is an important source of knowledge about mediaeval Poland, with descriptions of the economic, social and ethnic relations in Silesia. The Latin text of the Book contains the first known sentence written in Polish. The post-Cistercian monastery complex is a

**Henryków.
Cistercian abbey.**

on the left:

**Kłodzko. Gothic
bridge of St. John.**

Paczków. ▪▪
Gothic church
of St. John.

Paczków. ▪▪
Town hall.

on the right:
Nysa.
Church of St. James.

valuable architectural monument. The gently rolling plain of the Sudety Foothills includes several isolated massifs of hard crystalline rock (Mt. Ślęża and the Strzegomskie and Strzelińskie Hills), a source of valuable stone for house and road construction. One of the largest granite quarries is located in Strzelin.

Paczków on the Nysa Kłodzka, a tributary of the Odra, belongs to the most beautiful old towns in Silesia. Founded in 1254 by Tomasz, the Bishop of Wrocław, it was part of an episcopal "state". In 1428, it was captured by the Hussites, who for a time used it as a stronghold. The town flourished in the 16th century as a cloth-producing centre, exporting to Bohemia, Moravia and Austria. The loss of those markets in the 18th century, after annexation into Prussia, led to a decline of cloth production. Known as "the Silesian Carcasonne", Paczków escaped destruction during the second world war and retained the character of a typi-

cal mediaeval borough, encircled by walls with three gates and 19 bastions. The dominant edifices are a 14th-century Gothic defensive church with a massive tower and a Renaissance attic, and an impressive town hall from the mid-16th century, expanded and redesigned in the first half of the 19th century in the Classical style, and featuring an extant, 45 metre-high Renaissance tower. (I. J. K.)

The ancient Slav settlement of Nysa, which received municipal rights already in about 1220, lies on the south-western fringe of the voivodeship of Opole. From the 14th to the 17th century, it was a thriving cultural centre. In spite of immense wartime destruction, the parish church of St. Jacob, erected in 1392-1430 by Piotr of Ząbkowice as a great three-nave hall church with an ambulatory and adjoining chapels, remained unscathed. Lofty brick pillars with

Barycz river valley. Milickie Ponds.

on the right:

Kamieniec Ząbkowicki. Romantic castle according to a project by Karol Fryderyk Schinkel.

stone fillets define the view of the nave in a manner reminiscent of Italian Gothic churches. The Bohemian workshop of the Parlers left a vivid imprint. In the opinion of assorted scholars, the Nysa church appears to be a simplified version of St. Barbara's in Kutna Hora (Bohemia), whose construction was inaugurated by Peter Parler. The chapels, inserted between the buttresses, contain Gothic and Baroque tombstones and epitaphs of the bishops of Wrocław, the former owners of the borough. (P. T.)

The Chełm ridge, whose highest point is Mt. St. Anne (400 m), towers on the borderline between the Silesian Lowland and Upland. A huge amphitheatre was built amid the old basalt blocks at the foot of the

mountain. On top, there stands a Monument to the Silesian Insurgents, designed by Xawery Dunikowski and commemorating the battles waged in 1921 for the reunification of Opole Silesia with Poland.

Opole on the Odra, the ancient centre of the Opolanie tribe, is the capital of the region. A stronghold in the 10th century, it became the seat of a castellanship during the reign of Bolesław the Brave, and in 1202 assumed the function of the capital of a sovereign Piast duchy. In 1532, Opole was lost to the Habsburgs; it was pledged to Poland between 1645 and 1666, and from 1741 to 1945 remained under Prussian and then German rule. Trade and the crafts flourished under the Piasts; during the Prussian era,

the town became an important industrial centre. Despite the influx of Germans and the pressure of the Germanisation policy pursued by the authorities, the majority of the inhabitants of Opole retained their Polish identity. Badly damaged during World War II, the town had to be extensively reconstructed, particularly its historic centre. Opole possesses numerous monuments of sacral and lay architecture, including a 14th-century Gothic "Piast" tower (a remnant of the ducal castle) and a 15th-century collegiate church. Brzeg on the Odra lies on the eastern fringe of the Wrocław Plain. In 1234, a town replaced the 11th-century fortified castle-town and *suburbium*, and from 1311 to 1675 fulfilled the function of the capital of the independent duchy of Brzeg and Legnica. During its golden age in the 16th and 17th centuries Brzeg produced cloth and Gobelin tapestries. This was also the period of the construction of numerous Renaissance buildings and a thorough redesigning of the castle of the dukes of Brzeg (13th-14th centuries). The extant façade of the gatehouse, standing to the south of the castle, is opulently adorned with sculptures, including the figures of Jerzy II and Barbara, the ducal couple, encircled by two rows of busts of kings and dukes from the Piast dynasty. The interior displays a noteworthy polychrome mural depicting a genealogical tree composed of portraits. Today, the castle houses the Museum of the Silesian Piasts and plays host to numerous concerts (for example, the "Liszt Evenings" cycle and the Festival of Viennese Music). (I. J. K.)

Situated in the very heart of the Silesian Lowland, Wrocław is one of the oldest cities in Poland; for ten centuries, it remained the main historical centre of Silesia. The town grew on the site of an ancient settlement, the centre of the Ślężanie tribe dating back to the Stone Age. Incorporated into the Polish state in about 990, it must have played an important role since in 1000 Bolesław the Brave founded here one of the three bishoprics supervised by the Gniezno metropolitan see. The oldest castle-town was created on islets among the broads of the Odra. The seat of the dukes and bishops was established on Ostrów

fices were erected, usually replacing older buildings. They include the hall church of the Holy Virgin Mary on Piasek, whose interiors exemplify the Gothic architecture characteristic for Wrocław, and the church of the Holy Cross on Tum (1288-1350), one of the most valuable Gothic monuments in Poland; in the past, it contained the tomb of its founder, Duke Henry IV Probus, now in the National Museum. In 1526, Wrocław came under the rule of the Habsburgs, and from the 16th to the 18th century it acquired numerous Renaissance and Baroque buildings. As a Prussian town since 1741, subjected to increasing Germanisation, it remained a vigorous centre of Polish culture. In the inter-war period, the Polish community in Wrocław engaged in lively social and cultural activity, continued even at the time of the repressive measures taken by the Nazi authorities. The final battles of the second world war incurred grave losses to the besieged and fiercely defended town. Reconstructed Wrocław has become an important industrial city as well as a vital academic and cultural centre. (I. J. K.)

The church of St. Cross on Ostrów Tumski was founded in 1288 by Duke Henryk IV Probus, and completed in 1350. The two-level hall church, designed on a cruciform plan, is one of the few of its type in Europe. The eastern presbytery of the cathedral of St. John the Baptist from 1244-1272 is widely recognised as the first Gothic construction in Poland and a model for the cathedral on Cracow's Wawel Hill. The naves were erected in the first half of the 14th century, and the towers were completed during the 16th century. The siege in 1945 destroyed 70% of the cathedral, which has been carefully reconstructed. The two extant Baroque chapels are St. Elizabeth's (Jacopo Scianzi, 1680-1686) and the Electoral Chapel (the Austrian architect Hans B. Fischer von Erlach, 1715-1724), with polychrome and stucco executed by Italian artists.
The Wrocław town hall, similarly to many of its mediaeval counterparts, was created at the end of the 15th century by linking a row of houses into a single complex. The buildings, usually from the 14th

Wrocław. Interior of the church of the Holy Virgin Mary on Piasek.

on the right:
Wrocław. Cathedral, portal.

on pages 166-167:
Wrocław. Solny Square.

Tumski (the Tum Holm). Situated at the intersection of important trade routes, mediaeval Wrocław developed rapidly. Once the area of Ostrów Tumski and the adjacent Piaskowa Island proved to be too limited, the expanding town spread to the left bank of the Odra (turn of the 12th century). After the death of the last Piast ruler of Wrocław (1335), the town became incorporated into Bohemia. At the time, it was already one of the largest cities in Europe, and in the mid-14th century it belonged to the Hanseatic League. Numerous Gothic churches and secular edi-

century, were composed into a single, effective whole with rich sculptured decorations. Work was directed by Hans Berthold, and the team of sculptors included Paul Preusse, a colleague of the famous Arnold of Westphalia. The interiors house an exhibition of the city's history and the collections of the Medallion Art Museum. (P. T.)

At the turn of the 17th century, Silesia witnessed a significant architectural revival inspired by the Jesuits and other religious orders. Numerous Baroque objects appeared in Wrocław, until then an overwhelmingly Gothic city; two such buildings – a Jesuit collegiate church and a monastery of the Order of the Cross – were erected on the banks of the Odra. This was the period of the late phase of the Baroque, reflected in dynamic spatial solutions and picturesque interiors, elaborately ornamented with sculptures and paintings. The construction of the Jesuit collegiate church was commenced around 1728. Since 1811, this impressive building, often attributed to Johann Martinelli, houses the University. The assembly hall with the illusionistic *Apotheosis of Divine Wisdom* mural, numerous allegorical sculptures and paintings is a good illustration of a Late Baroque interior. (P. T.)

The other Baroque façade reflected in the Odra waters is that of the former monastery of the Order of the Cross, built in 1675-1715 as a three-winged palace linked with a domed lower building. The author of the design was probably the French architect Jean-Baptiste Mathieu, who also planned the Prague church of this monastic order. The Wrocław edifice is more compact and possesses stronger Classical forms than other Baroque buildings in Central Europe. Today, it houses the Ossoliński National Institute, an important Polish cultural centre founded in 1817 in Lvov, which amasses and studies valuable monuments of Polish literature and acts as a publishing house. In addition, the Ossolineum possesses extensive prints, numismatic and medal collections. (P. T.)

on the left:

**Wrocław.
University,
Aula Leopoldina.**

examples of 19th-century Polish painting and contemporary art. Silesian ceramics and glass, for centuries manufactured in the province, are also well represented. The Museum organised a unique section devoted to the art of the book, the only of its sort in Poland. The Medallion Art Museum in the town hall gathers Polish and foreign medals from the 16th century to modern times. The Archdiocesan Museum possesses a rich collection of Silesian Gothic art, part of which is exhibited in the Holy Virgin Mary church on Piasek. Wrocław has the only Museum of Architecture in Poland, housed in the historic buildings of the former Bernardine monastery and church from the turn of the 15th century. (P. T.)

The town of Oleśnica was built on a trade route from Wrocław to Greater Poland. Already during the 11th century, it was preceded by a ducal castle-town and a trading settlement. In 1240, Duke Henry II of Wrocław replaced the stronghold with a castle, which in the 16th century was remodelled into a Renaissance palace. A separate duchy of Oleśnica was created in 1312. After the death of the last representative of the local Piast dynasty (1492), the town passed into the hands of the Bohemian Podiebrads, and then, in 1647, the dukes of Wirtemberg. Oleśnica was a vital publishing centre of the 16th-century Polish Protestant movement. Cotton-spinning developed in the 18th century, and industry was introduced after a railway line was built in the second half of the 19th century. During World War II, some 80% of the town was destroyed. Upon its restoration to Poland in 1945, rebuilt Oleśnica emerged as an industrial centre; it also serves the neighbouring farming areas. The town holds two mass-scale events: the Days of Oleśnica, organised at the beginning of June, and the Days of Europe in early September. (I. J. K.)

The ancient tribal centre and market settlement of Trzebnica, picturesquely situated among hills, received municipal rights in the mid-13th century. In 1202, Duke Henry the Bearded founded and richly endowed the first Cistercian convent in Silesia. From

J. Styka, *Polonia*, 1891, National Museum in Wrocław.

on the right:
Oleśnica. Ducal castle.

The largest collections of works of art in Wrocław are to be found in the National Museum, opened in 1947 in an almost totally ruined city whose resources had been reduced to a fraction of their former greatness. Part of the present collections originates from the prewar museums of Lvov. Special value is ascribed to the exhibition of Silesian mediaeval art and Baroque sculpture. The Museum also possesses valuable

that time on, the history of the town and the abbey was closely linked: during the fifteenth century, both were plundered by the Hussites, and after the Thirty Years War the reconstruction of the borough (in the Late Baroque style) was accompanied by the erection of a new abbey. Unfortunately, in 1810 all monasteries and convents in Prussia fell prey to cassation. In the 16th-18th century, Trzebnica became a centre of linen production, followed in the 18th century by cloth. The Spring of St. Jadwiga spa, opened at the

Moszna. Palace.

on the left:

Trzebnica. Church of St. Jadwiga of Silesia.

close of the 19th century, still welcomes visitors. Despite numerous conflagrations and wartime devastation (including the damage suffered during the second world war) Trzebnica has preserved a post-Cistercian monastic complex, one of the most valuable historical monuments of architecture in Poland, together with a 13th-century Gothic church (today: the basilica of St. Jadwiga) and the crypt of St. Bartholomew underneath the presbytery. The wide river valley of the Odra was once overgrown by magnificent marshland forests with a dense undergrowth. Scarce remnants of those woods have survived in the regions of Raciborz, Koźle, Oława, Wrocław, Wołów and Środa Śląska. (I. J. K.)

The Benedictine abbey in Legnickie Pole, one of the most beautiful Late Baroque buildings in Poland, was built in 1727-1731 according to a design by Kilian Ignaz Dientzenhofer, the author of many important objects in Prague, such as the church of St. Michael in the Old Town and the church of the Ursuline order on the Hradshin. Dientzenhofer sought new spatial solutions, with a predilection for plans consisting of interconnecting circles and ellipses to lend the interiors a unique, dynamic fluidity. This was the sort of plan used in the church of St. Jadwiga, built for Bohemian Benedictines on the site of a great battle waged with the Tartars in 1241, which claimed the life of Henry the Pious, the Piast Duke of Silesia. Wenceslas Lawrence Reiner, another Prague artist, executed the paintings, while those adorning the altar are the work of Francis de Backer from Antwerp. The magnificent polychrome from 1733 is by Cosmas Damian Asam of Munich.

The Cistercian abbey at Lubiąż, built in 1690-1720, is one of the great monastic complexes in Silesia. The late 18th-century Baroque fragments of the church, engulfed by a façade stretching almost a quarter of a kilometre, conceal Gothic walls from the early 14th century. The monastery contains a well-preserved, splendid library with polychrome decorations by Christian F. Bentum, and a ducal hall from 1734-1738, whose richly painted and sculptured embellishment was envisaged as a glorification of the Habsburg dynasty. (P. T.)

Legnica on the Kaczawa is another old centre in the voivodeship of Lower Silesia. At the beginning of the 13th century it was the site of a ducal palatium with a chapel, the seat of Duke Henry the Bearded, which gave way to a castle redesigned in the first half of the sixteenth century in the Renaissance spirit.

The Late Renaissance gate from 1533 is the outcome of this achitectural venture and the enclosure of the castle by earthworks with bastions and a moat. Further refashioning and fires (the largest in 1835 and 1945) lay waste the magnificent bulding, reconstructed in the 1960s.

In the southern part of the voivodeship of Lubusz lies Żagań, founded in the 12th century by Duke Bolesław IV the Curly. The palace, of Italian workmanship, was erected for Prince Albrecht Wallenstein in 1628 as a Mannerist residence, and was redesigned after 1648 for Prince von Lobkovic by the architect Antonio della Porta. The simple monumental façade with a rusticated socle and vertical divisions emulates Bernini. (P.T.)

Środa Śląska. Houses in market square.

on the left:

Legnica. Cathedral of St. Peter and Paul.

The Greater Poland Lowland

The Greater Poland Lowland is the cradle of the Polish state. It was here that the oldest strongholds of the Polanie tribe grew in the 8th and 9th century. This nucleus of Polish statehood is an area of ancient settlements dating back to the Neolithic Age. Their numerous vestiges include Biskupin near Żnin, in the voivodeship of Kujawy-Pomerania, a monument of international importance; the fortified settlement from the period of Lusatian culture (Early Iron Age, about 730 B. C.) was discovered in 1933 on a peninsula (formerly, an island) on Lake Biskupin. Excavations revealed the ground plan of the settlement, while the unearthed objects made it possible to reconstruct the life of the inhabitants – about 1 000 persons subsisting on agriculture and animal husbandry. The findings also encompassed remains of artisan workshops. Several houses and a fragment of the rampart with a gate and a breakwater have been reconstructed. From 1995, Biskupin is the site of an annually held Archaeological Festival, with lectures, demonstrations of experimental archaeology, and stagings of battles waged by ancient warriors as well as equally prehistoric rites. (I. J. K.)

One of the localities associated with the emergence of Polish statehood is Ostrów Lednicki, an island on Lake Lednica with traces of a settlement from the Mesolithic Age. During the 9th and 10th century, a third of the island was occupied by a stronghold surrounded by high ramparts, which today contains the remains of a stone palatium. According to tradition, this was the birthplace of Bolesław the Brave, the first crowned King of Poland. (I. J. K.)

Gniezno was the first capital of the Polish state united by Mieszko I. Its name is derived from the eagle's

on the right:

Biskupin. View of a wooden turret over an entrance to the settlement.

nest (Polish: *gniazdo*) found by Lech, the legendary ancestor of the Poles. In the year 1000, Emperor Otto III, sumptuously received by Bolesław the Brave, visited Gniezno as a pilgrim to the tomb of Bishop Wojciech (Adalbert), who lost his life during a mission in Pruthenia and was canonised soon after. This was the time of the foundation of the Gniezno archbishopric and metropolitan see, which in 1025 was the site of the coronation of Duke Bolesław. The political role of the town diminished after its devastation during the Bohemian invasion of 1038; nonetheless, it remained – and has until today – the historic seat of the Church authorities in Poland.

The Old Town has retained its urban layout and multiple historical monuments. The oldest, a pre-Romanesque church, burned down in 1018 and was replaced by Bolesław the Brave who erected a Romanesque church. In the 17th and 18th century, the Gothic cathedral, built in 1342-1372 on the foundations of its predecessor, was remodelled and encircled by Renaissanceand Baroque chapels. The cathedral, destroyed in a fire in 1945, has been rebuilt in its old form. The most valuable among the numerous relics are the Romanesque bronze doors (about 1170), with bas-reliefs showing scenes from the life and death of St. Adalbert. (I. J. K.)

Gniezno.
Interior of the cathedral
with the sepulchre
of St. Wojciech.

on the left:

Poznań. Cathedral.

Gniezno.
Cathedral, fragment
of the Gniezno Door.

Poznań, the chief city of the Greater Poland Lowland, is situated in the Warta river valley at the very spot where the river can be crossed, an ancient settlement site dating back to the end of the Stone Age. A stronghold, with a *suburbium* nestling below, was built in the 9th century on Ostrów Tumski (the Tum Holm) between the Warta and its tributary, the Cybina. The mythical founder was Poznan, who gave his name to the town. In the mid-10th century, the stronghold was enlarged and transformed into a powerful fortress, from which Mieszko I set off on expeditions against the region of Lubusz and Western Pomerania. Poznań shared with Gniezno the functions of the favourite ducal seat, and from 968 – the rank of Poland's first bishopric. Destroyed in the course of the Bohemian invasion, the castle-town, rebuilt during the fragmentation of the country into feudal provinces, became the capital of the Greater Poland line of the Piast dynasty. The town began to expand: in 1230, a settlement on the right bank of the Cybina, known as Śródka, was granted municipal status. Since neither Śródka nor Ostrów Tumski could expand due to limited space, Duke Przemysław I transferred the economic centre to the left bank of the Warta. In 1253, a *locatio* of left-bank Poznań was performed in accordance with Magdeburg law. A castle and defence walls, encircling the town, were built at the end of the 13th century, followed by a Gothic town hall (turn of

on the right:
Poznań.
Ostrów Tumski.

the 13th century). Granted numerous privileges, Poznań grew rapidly and outpaced Gniezno to become the main urban centre of Greater Poland. In addition, it was crossed by trade routes from Mazovia, Lithuania and Rus' to Leipzig and Nuremburg as well as from Cracow to Szczecin. Already during the 15th century, it assumed the role of a large trading centre, known throughout Europe for the St. John fair. At the time of its golden age, Poznań concentrated the majority of Polish import and the whole of transit trade between the East and the West. It was also a centre of the crafts, culture and the medical sciences. The Lubrański Academy, founded here in 1519, was the second oldest school of higher learning in Poland. Printing and the book trade evolved. The Reformation left a distinct imprint upon 16th-century Poznań. The town expanded and altered its appearance; new suburbs arose and numerous buildings were constructed, including the residences and palaces of the nobility and magnates. (L. J. K.)

The official adoption of Christianity by Poland in 966 was followed by the construction of a monumental cathedral on Ostrów Tumski. The cathedral, whose fragments have survived in the vaults of the present-day building, was patterned after imperial foundations, and its form was reminiscent of Benedictine churches in the West. A new, Romanesque cathedral was constructed in 1058-1079 after the devastation incurred during the Bohemian invasion. The Gothic cathedral from 1346-1428 emulated Pomeranian and Silesian architecture, although some of the solutions resembled those applied in French cathedrals. The choir was built together with an ambulatory, typical for cathedrals, and assured additional lighting by lantern turrets placed above the three spans of the ambulatory, thus fundamentally altering the eastern part of the solid. The ambulatory opens onto three chapels; in time, the central chapel was remodelled into the Golden Chapel. In 1815-1840, the latter chapel was granted a Romantic-Byzantine appearance in an attempt to commemorate Mieszko I and Bolesław the Brave, buried in the cathedral. Designed by the architect Francesco M. Lanci and

the sculptor Christian Rauch, the construction, funded thanks to resources donated by the people of Greater Poland, reflects a carefully conceived historic and national programme intent on creating a patriotic sanctuary for Poles living in the Prussian partition area. The shape of the chapel was to refer to the pre-Romanesque rotunda on Ostrów Lednicki, which at that time was being examined and was considered a palatium of the first Piasts. At the time, the Byzantine style was regarded as indigenous for Polish art from the Piast era. The figure of the Creator of the Universe and likenesses of the saints, surrounded by the coats of arms of various illustrious families and bishops, adorn the chapel interiors to express the conviction that Poland had been created by feudal lords and churchmen. A copy of Titian's *Assunta* installed in the altar was additionally enhanced with the inscription: *Bogu Rodzica Dziewica*, the opening words of *Bogurodzica* (The Mother of God), an old Polish knights' hymn. Two other paintings portray Mieszko I toppling pagan deities and Otto III with Bolesław the Brave at the sepulchre of St. Adalbert. The figure of Bolesław was given the facial features of Prince Józef Poniatowski, a modern national hero. The Golden Chapel exemplifies those works of art which fulfilled essential ideological functions in a society deprived of its independence. (P. T.)

In 1508, the old, Gothic town hall (from the turn of the 13th century) in the Market Square was expanded (arcades) prior to a fundamental remodelling in the Renaissance style (1550-1560): new interior decoration, the addition of a loggia and attics, as well as sgrafitto and polychrome murals on the façade. A Neoclassical tower was added in 1781-1783. The arcaded Late Gothic-Renaissance town houses of the local stallkeepers, standing next to the town hall, also date from the 15th-17th century; the majority was subsequently granted Baroque and Classicist façades.
During the Enlightenment, when trade grew and manufacturing was inaugurated (mainly textile mills), Poznań began to recover from a decline

on the left:

**Poznań.
Renaissance town hall
built according
to a project by
Jan Baptysta Quadro.**

Poznań. The Raczyński Library.

caused by wars raging in the 17th century. After the second partition of Poland (1793), the town shared the fate of the whole of Greater Poland and fell under Prussian rule. In 1807-1815, it enjoyed the status of the capital of a department in the Duchy of Warsaw. In the wake of the Congress of Vienna (1815), the borough was once again incorporated into Prussia and assumed the rank of the capital of the Grand Duchy of Poznań, subsequently deprived

of its autonomy as reprisal for the Greater Poland Uprising of 1848. At the time, Poznań became an important scientific and cultural centre, involved in propagating Polish political and social thought. A library was founded by Edward Raczyński in 1829, and the ensuing years witnessed the establishment of printing houses and the Poznań Society of Friends of Science. After the failed uprising, Polish society effectively opposed the Germanisation campaign

rated into the borough. Further opportunities for progress were severely curtailed by the erection of a fortress with a citadel, fortification and ramparts (1829-1839); the whole complex was liquidated as late as 1900, paving the way for further urban development. The first world war raised hopes of regaining independence. The Greater Poland Uprising, which broke out on 27 December 1918, led to the liberation of Poznań and then spread across the whole of Greater Poland. Throughout the inter-war years, Poznań, now a voivodeship capital, continued to grow. Poznań University was opened in 1919, followed by four other schools of higher learning, and Poznań became one of the key scientific and cultural centres in the country. In the economy pride of place still went to trade, as evidenced by the Poznań Fair, organised since 1921, and in 1925 transformed into an international event echoing the mediaeval traditions of the celebrated St. John fair.

During the second world war, Poznań and Greater Poland were incorporated into the Nazi Reich as the so-called Wartheland or Warthegau. The German occupation comprised the most tragic stage in the history of the town, bringing arrests, deportations and the destruction of Polish national monuments. Despite raging terror Poznań remained a Resistance centre, involved in constant Intelligence and sabotage campaigns. The losses suffered during the last stage of the war totalled 55 % of the whole town and as much as 80% of the historic City. Thanks to their traditional organisational talents and industrious nature the inhabitants of Poznań needed only five years to rebuild the town and embark upon its expansion. A new central district and residential estates sprung up, and the communication system was remodelled. Industry advanced, and today the International Fair, now a global event, attracts exhibitors and traders from all over the world. New schools of higher education and scientific institutes were opened, and the Society of Friends of Science revived its activity, interrupted by the war. Cultural and artistic life blossomed. The Polish Theatre (opened already in 1875) enjoys high acclaim, and the opera house and philharmonic are among the

conducted by the ruling authorities. This was a period of economic growth, with a predominant role played by trade, the crafts and industry, linked primarily with food processing and services offered to the thriving agriculture of the region. The 19th century brought considerable territorial expansion. After the secularisation of Church property in 1797, terrains in the vicinity of Poznań, previously subjected to Church and monastic jurisdiction, were incorpo-

on the right:

Poznań.

Market square.

country's best. The S. Stuligrosz Boys' and Men's Choir of the State Philharmonic has won international acclaim; the same is true of the "Amadeus" Chamber Orchestra conducted by Agnieszka Duczmal. The restored buildings, which in numerous cases were granted their original appearance, are largely concentrated in the Old Town and on Ostrów Tumski, where the mediaeval street layout has been preserved. Examples of historic sacral and lay architecture are to be found in the former suburbs. The monuments of Poznań, meticulously rebuilt and frequently reconstructed, constitute a considerable tourist attraction. (I. J. K.)

The local museums – Archaeological, Archdiocesan and of Musical Instruments – feature fascinating and varied collections. The exhibits displayed in the National Museum showrooms date back to 1857, and include numerous excellent examples of Polish art from the Middle Ages to recent years as well as important paintings from assorted European schools: Italian (primarily from the 16th century), Dutch (17th century) and Spanish (the most valuable collection of its sort in Poland). Masterpieces of European crafts are featured separately. Museum departments are housed in palaces in Rogalin, Gołuchów and Śmiełów. (P. T.)

The post-Jesuit church was constructed for many years: begun in 1649-1653, it was not completed until 1732 (the façade). A whole pleiad of monastic architects was supervised by Bartłomiej Wąsowski; the majority were Italians, and Wąsowski himself had travelled to Italy. It is not surprising, therefore, that the resultant edifice clearly echoed Roman ecclesiastical architecture, and contains the most superlative Baroque interiors in Poland, a perfect synthesis of architecture, painting and sculpture. In the manner of theatrical wings the massive, deep red columns direct the visitor's gaze towards the lavishly illuminated altar. In spite of the protracted period of construction the outcome complies with a remarkably consistent vision, enhancing the effect of pathos and monumentality. (P. T.)

on pages 190-191:

Rogalin.

The Raczyński Palace,

garden elevation.

In the past, Rogalin, located 17 km south of Poznań on the bank of the Warta, was the estate of a knight. From the 18th century until the second world war, it belonged to the Raczyński family, whose members were widely-known patrons of the arts. The Baroque-Classical castle from 1770-1782, connected with its outbuildings by means of two galleries, possesses beautiful Classicistic interiors, including a drawing room and ground floor designed by Domenico Merlini, and a staircase by Johann C. Kamsetzer. Separate rooms were constructed in 1909-1910 to display a collection of Polish and European paintings from the 19th and early 20th century. During the Nazi occupation, the palace was methodically looted by the Germans. Today, its main body houses a department of the National Museum in Poznań, featuring an exhibition of palace interiors from the 17th-19th century; the painting gallery contains part of the former collections amassed by Edward Raczyński. The carriage house is used for keeping a collection of about twenty horsedrawn carriages, once the property of the palace. The surrounding is composed of a geometrical and landscape park designed in the French-Dutch style, and an English garden stretching beyond, with former estate buildings and the Classicist chapel of St. Marcel from 1820, a copy of a Roman temple (the so-called Maison Carrée) in Nîmes. The chapel interior includes the Raczyński family mausoleum designed in the Romantic Gothic style. The park boasts of the largest complex of centuries-old oaks in Poland (with a circumference of up to 9 m), of which 954 are protected as monuments of nature. (I. J. K.)

The town of Kórnik, situated to the south-east of Poznań, owes its fame to the museum and library founded in 1839 by Tytus Działyński in a 16th-century castle (built on the site of an older wooden castle from 1426). The castle was erected for the Górka family, the then owners of Kórnik, and redesigned in 1845-1860 in the Romantic Gothic style. The museum of period interiors contains a priceless collection of furniture, paintings, sculptures, artifacts, arms, armour and hunting trophies, together with ethnographic, archaeological and natural science collections from Poland and abroad. A historic outbuilding, the so-called Prowenta, is the birthplace of Wisława Szymborska, winner of the Nobel Prize in literature. The library, composed of more than 150 000 volumes, contains Polish prints from the 16th-17th century, valuable manuscripts and cartographic collections, property of the Polish Academy of Sciences. In 1925, Władysław Zamoyski, the last owner of Kórnik, presented the castle together with the collections, library, landed estates and the Działyński Palace in Poznań as a gift to the Polish nation, creating a foundation known as the Kórnik Enterprise. The castle park was laid out during the 16th century in the Italian style; later, it became converted into a French park and then

Kórnik.
Castle redesigned
in 1846-1861 in the
Neo-Gothic style
upon the initiative of
Tytus Działyński.

on the left:

Famous oak trees
in Rogalin.

granted the features of a 19th-century English garden. Tytus Działyński initiated the acclimatisation of exotic trees and shrubs, a task continued by his son, Jan Kanty. Today, this is the largest dendrological park in Poland, with about 10 000 varieties of domestic and tropical trees and shrubs. (I. J. K.)

The region of Lake Gopło, the largest lake in Greater Poland, abounds in legends and myths explaining the origins of the Polish state. Here, angels supposedly greeted the wheelwright Piast, a possible analogy to the Biblical story of Abraham. Legends also describe how the evil ruler Popiel was devoured by mice in a lakeside tower. Gopło is the setting for Słowacki's *Lila Weneda* and *Balladyna*, Kraszewski's *Stara baśń* (*The Ancient Tale*) and Żeleński's opera *Goplana*. Although the Mouse Tower is actually part of a 14th-century castle built by Kazimierz the Great, archaeologists continue to discover in it numerous traces of an earlier settlement. Today, the lake stretches for about 25 km; in second century A. D., at the time of the Roman amber trade route, it was more than 40 km long. Roman traders were familiar with Kruszwica as a prominent settlement, which in the 8th-9th century evolved into a defensive stronghold. The three-nave Romanesque collegiate church from 1120-1140 is the town's most treasured historic monument. The particularly harmonious eastern end of the building is closed by five semi-circular apses, rendering it similar to Benedictine churches in Western Europe. (P. T.)

An exceptional complex of Romanesque architecture has been preserved in Strzelno, located in the Gniezno Lake District. The buildings include the rotunda of St. Prokop from the second half of the 12th century with an extremely interesting interior, and the adjoining Premonstratensian convent church of the Holy Trinity, in which the walls between the naves are supported by Romanesque columns discovered in 1946 during the removal of Baroque stoning. The shafts of two columns are entirely decorated with figural bas-relief. Figures in the arcades symbolise human virtues and vices as envisaged in mediaeval moral treatises – a depiction unique in European

art. Other extant examples of Romanesque sculpture reflect the former splendour of the church. (P. T.)

The town of Inowrocław, situated on the surrounding plain, was known already during the 11th century as a settlement which held fairs, and the property of the dukes of Mazovia. The Romanesque church of the Holy Virgin Mary was built at the beginning of the 13th cen-

Strzelno. Rotunda of St. Prokop.

on the left:

Kruszwica. Romanesque collegiate church, view from the east.

tury as a single-nave edifice with two towers. The northern elevation is composed of granite blocks; those next to the portal are adorned with stone-carved masks which probably fulfilled a magical function. The main altar features the so-called *Smiling Madonna* –14th-century Gothic sculpture. (P. T.)

Alongside fertile soil, salt is the most important natural resource of the Kujawy region. Salt springs – the largest in the village of Ciechocinek – were discovered at the end of the 18th century. Further search was con-

Inowrocław.
Stone masks
in the wall of a
Romanesque church.

on the left:

Inowrocław.
Church of the Holy
Virgin Mary.

Bydgoszcz. Granary on the river Brda.

ducted by the government of the Kingdom of Poland after Ciechocinek was purchased from its private owners (1823). In 1822-1828 and 1859, three graduation towers, used up to this day, were built for the purposes of a spa. A pump room was added in 1859. Today, Ciechocinek is one of the leading health resorts and spas in Poland. (I. J. K.)

Bydgoszcz, the capital of the Kujawy-Pomerania voiovodeship, derives its origin from a mediaeval fortified stronghold and later a castle-town, which guarded the passageway across the swampy valley of the Vistula. The town prospered considerably in the 15th and 16th century thanks to the wheat, timber and salt trade. Large granaries from the 18th and 19th century recall its mercantile functions. During the partition era, Bydgoszcz, under Prussian rule, was subjected to an intensive Germanisation campaign which also involved the destruction of historical monuments attesting to the town's Polish character; the castle and numerous sacral and lay buildings were demolished. The inter-war expansion of Byd-

goszcz was halted by the second world war; Nazi occupation began with mass-scale executions and a deportation of the local population. Rapid post-1945 development was connected predominantly with industry. Bydgoszcz also became a major administrative, cultural and academic centre. (I. J. K.)

The attractive tourist area of the Łagów Lake District includes the Łagów Landscape Park, opened in 1985. Lake Łagów, with its high embankments and ravines shrouded with deciduous woods, is perhaps the most beautiful of the numerous lakes in the region. It is linked with the larger and equally impressive Lake Ciecz. The town of Łagów, a favourite tourist destination, is situated on an isthmus between the two lakes. The 12th-century castle-town became the property of Brandenburg in the mid-13th century; in 1299-1346, it was a knights' fief and then, until 1810, it belonged to a commandery of the Knights of Malta, who early in the 14th century built a massive castle with a 35 m-high tower. After the restoration of Łagów to Poland, the castle,

- **Łagów.**
  Castle of the
  Joannite knights'
  order.

- **Łagów.**
  The Polska Gate
  from the 15th
  century.

Inowłódz. Romanesque church of St. Giles, end of the 11th century.

seriously damaged in 1945, was rebuilt and adapted to serve as a hotel with a restaurant and a cafe. (I. J. K.)

Zielona Góra lies in a basin amid the moraine hills of the Zielona Góra Elevation. The town, which probably evolved in the second half of the 13th century out of a much older agrarian settlement at the cross-roads of trade routes between Wrocław and Szczecin, was granted municipal rights in 1323. At the time, it was part of the duchy of Głogów-Żagań, ruled until 1488 by Piast dukes who from the middle of the 14th century were the vassals of the Bohemian Crown and in the 15th century – of Hungary. In 1490, the whole of Silesia became the demesne of Ladislas

Jagiellon, the King of Hungary and Bohemia, who granted the duchy of Głogów to his two brothers, later Polish monarchs: to Jan Olbracht (in 1491) and Zygmunt (in 1498). In 1506, the duchy was incorporated into Bohemia. The town developed during the particularly conducive 15th and 16th century thanks to the production of cloth and wine from vineyards cultivated already in the 13th century. In 1742, Zielona Góra, together with the whole of Lower Silesia, fell under Prussian rule. The production of wine declined; today, it is continued on a limited scale and the annual Grape Harvest Festival, held every September, draws tourists from all over the country. Zielona Góra remained a centre of cloth production,

Zielona Góra.

Market Square.

**Rakoniewice.
Arcaded houses.**

and the 19th century witnessed the growth of the metallurgical and machine-building industries. After the second world war, the town, now a voivodeship capital, developed as an industrial and cultural centre. The oldest historical monuments in Zielona Góra include the Łazienna Tower, also known as the Głodowa (Hunger) Tower, a remnant of a gatehouse from 1487; remodelled upon numerous occasions, it is topped with a Baroque cupola and lantern. The history of the noteworthy cathedral of St. Jadwiga goes back to the 13th century. As a result of assorted fires and redesigning ventures the present-day building contains elements of diverse styles. The interior features a well-preserved Baroque choir and a number of tombstones. (I . J. K.)

Greater Poland offers an opportunity to encounter numerous vestiges of timber architecture, such as those in Rakoniewice, a small town in the Poznań Lake District and a centre of the local farming

on the right:
Leszno. Town hall.

region. Prior to its incorporation into Prussia (1772) Rakoniewice was known for craft and trading, evidenced by extant arcaded wooden houses, once belonging to the town's artisans. The nearby town of Buk has an interesting 18th-century Baroque cemetery church of the Holy Cross (skeleton construction). (I. J. K.).

The town of Leszno, ensconced by coniferous woods and located in the historical Wschowa region on the borderland between Greater Poland and Silesia, was the object of rivalry between the local dukes. In 1343, Kazimierz the Great resolved the controversy, and the region became part of Greater Poland. At the turn of the 14th century, Leszno was the property of the Wieniawita knights, who adopted the name of Leszczyński from the locality. In 1547, the borough was granted municipal status, and in the mid-16th century it became a centre of the Reformation and a refuge for the Bohemian Brethren, who fled from

persecution in the Catholic Habsburg monarchy. Rafał Leszczyński, a sympathiser of the Reformation, settled the Brethren on his estates. The Leszczyński family also initiated the foundation of a Protestant school (1555), which in 1626 was granted the rank of a secondary school. For many years, one of its teachers was Jan Amos Komensky, a famous progressive pedagogue, writer, philosopher and theologian, who arrived together with a group of Bohemians and Moravians. In approximately 1633, a Lutheran community came into being. At the time, Leszno was a significant cultural and publishing centre. In 1655, the Protestant inhabitants of Leszno openly welcomed Swedish invaders; a year later, they paid a terrible price for this act of support for their co-religionists when Polish troops set fire to the town in revenge. Rapidly rebuilt and flourishing, Leszno became a centre of the crafts, especially cloth and tanning, and trade. The impact of the Reformation gradually waned. In the early 18th century, Leszno belonged to Stanisław Leszczyński, twice elected King of Poland and the father of Maria Leszczyńska, the wife of Louis XV of France; ultimately, Leszczyński was forced into exile by the Russians. In 1738, Leszno was purchased by the Sułkowski family, and in 1797 it was incorporated into the Prussian partition area. Cloth production was no match for Russian competition, although other crafts, trade and the processing industry continued to progress. Between the world wars, Leszno was a thriving economic centre of southern Greater Poland, a role it continues to play today. Devastated upon many occasions, it has nevertheless retained its mediaeval layout and several historical monuments, including the magnificent Baroque town hall rebuilt after a fire by the eminent Italian architect Pompeo Ferrari at the beginning of the 18th century. (I. J. K.).

The small historic town of Osieczna on Lake Łoniewskie, 10 km north-east of Leszno, is a regional crafts and services centre, as well as a spa with impressive bathing facilities. The most highly prized of the 15th-- 19th-century buildings are three wooden windmills from the later half of the 18th century.

on the left:

Rydzyna.

The Leszczyński Palace.

on the right:

Osieczna.

Wooden windmills.

Standing in a picturesque cluster on a hillock they evoke the landscape of the Spanish province of La Mancha. (I. J. K.)

The small town of Rydzyna to the south-east of Leszno has a Baroque layout, whose main axis is a street linking the market square with the residence of the former owners. Foremost among the numerous historical monuments is the Baroque palace of the Leszczyński family, erected in 1685-1695 on the Gothic foundations and, partially, walls of a 15th-century castle belonging to the Rydzyński family. In about 1700, the west wing of the palace was redesigned by the Italian architect Pompeo Ferrari, who lived in Rydzyna from the end of the 17th century to his death in 1736. Burned down during the Northern War, the palace was rebuilt and remodelled in 1742-1745 by Karl M. Frantz, employed by Aleksander J. Sułkowski, a successive owner. A park designed on a geometrical plan was laid out in the 17th century. In 1762, August Sułkowski founded a Piarist academy to which he bequeathed his whole estate in case of the extinction of his family. After the death of the last Sułkowski, the Rydzyna estate was seized by the Prussian authorities, and it was not until the inter-war period that the "Sułkowski Foundation" was set up; in 1928, an experimental boarding school was opened in the palace. Today, the palace, rebuilt after a fire (1945), houses a Centre for Technical Progress. (I. J. K.)

Amidst the exotic trees of the sprawling landscape park in Gołuchów, on the Kalisz Elevation, there stands a Romantic castle built in the style of the French Renaissance, and redesigned in 1875-1885 to accommodate a museum. In about 1560, this was the site of a fortified manor house which at the beginning of the 17th century was transformed by Wacław Leszczyński, the voivode of Poznań, into an impressive palace. By the 19th century, the residence had become a ruin, which its successive owners, Jan Działyński and his wife, Izabella, born Czartoryska, rebuilt to house their extensive art collections, including priceless Greek vases, primarily

on pages 208-209:

Gołuchów.

Castle in the French

Renaissance style

Gostyń.
Church of the
Philippine order,
interior of the dome.

black- and red-figure vessels from Attica. The construction was entrusted to French artists, and the sculptured decoration, predominantly 16th-century objects, came from demolished French and Italian monuments. The courtyard walls featured fragments of bas-reliefs, mosaics and medallions, including a portrait of a resident of Palmyra. After the rich art treasures were dispersed as a result of wartime perturbations the castle became part of the National Museum in Poznań; the subsequent series of period interiors contains a number of preserved fireplaces and portals bearing the date of 1619, once the property of the Leszczyński palace. Another local tourist attraction is the largest erratic boulder in Greater

Poland, grey Scandinavian granite known as the rock of St. Kinga (with a circumference of 22 m). (P. T.)

One of the particularly noteworthy landmarks in Gostyń, a town in the Leszno Elevation, is the Baroque church of the Philippine order. When in 1676 Zofia, born Opalińska, visited Venice she was so enchanted by Santa Maria della Salute, the church built by Baldassare Longhena on the Grand Canal, that upon returning to Gostyń she requested that this masterpiece be recreated by the Italian architect Giorgio Catenaci. The nave, based on an octagonal plan, was built in 1679-1698 and completed in 1726-1728 by Pompeo Ferrari, who raised the dome on a huge drum and enclosed the presbytery. Ferrari, who married and settled down in Poland, was the author of numerous buildings in Greater Poland, all attesting to his great talent. The intrados of the dome, similarly to his work in Ląd, was decorated with frescoes by the acclaimed Silesian painter Georg W. Neunhertz, who in 1745-1746 illustrated the history of St. Philip, the patron of the order. The frescoes reveal an impressive freedom of composition and brilliant arrangements of succulent, lively colours. (P. T.)

At the end of the 16th century and during the first half of the 17th century, the Polish gentry built brick manor houses which combined Italian Mannerism with local, traditional forms. One such example, found in Poddębice, the seat of Zygmunt Grudziński, the voivode of Rawa, was erected in 1610-1617. The freely composed elevation consists of a tower, a staircase and a two-storey loggia with flattened arches. A triangular gable above the cornice is richly embellished with irregularly arranged pinnacles. Both the gable and the stucco decoration of the loggia vaulting are typical for Polish Mannerism. (P. T.)

Already in the second century A. D. the Roman geographer Ptolemy mentioned Kalisz (Calissia), one Poland's oldest towns, as an important stop along the amber trail. In the 16th and 17th century, the town prospered as a linen manufacturing centre. Here, the Jesuits built one of their first churches in Poland (1587-1595). The majority of the stately buildings, however, dates from the early 19th century, and was designed in the Neoclassical spirit by Sylwester Szpilowski (for example, the seat of the Tribunal – the district court). (P. T.)

The town of Jarocin on the Kalisz Elevation developed from a ducal market settlement and in 1257 received municipal rights from Bolesław the Pious, the Duke of Greater Poland. Growth was associated with trade and the crafts. After a period of decline caused by the wars of the 17th and 18th century, the borough recovered in the second half of the 19th

century. Today, it is an important road and railway junction, as well as an industrial centre. Despite frequent devastation, Jarocin managed to preserve a number of historical monuments, such as the arcaded town hall from 1799-1804. The charming park designed by Piotr Józef Lenne includes ancient oak trees and a unique hornbeam alley, one of longest in Europe. (I. J. K.)

One of the best preserved wooden manor houses can be found in Ożarów. Built in 1757 by Władysław Bartochowski of the Rola coat of arms, it features a typical shingled mansard roof. The stone-brick founda-

Kalisz. Town hall.

tion supports a frame construction made of larch beams. Four alcoves were designed in the corners of the house, which today contains a Museum of Manorial Interiors. The extensive activity of the Museum encompasses annual Ethnological Colloquia, concerts and meetings devoted to folklore. As residences of the gentry, manor houses played a significant role in Polish history and culture. The tradition of the manor house, conceived as the characteristic dwelling of the Polish landowner, was upheld to the beginning of the 20th century. The wooden church in Grębień, several kilometres to the east of Ożarów, features a unique polychrome decoration of the beamed ceiling. The church was built around 1500, and twenty years later its interior was enhanced with paintings which departed from the tradition of floral patterns whose purpose was to transform the ceiling into the garden of Paradise. In Grębień, luxuriant plant tendrils, known from Renaissance graphic art, are peopled by musicians – courtly with a lute, and rural with a fiddle. (P. T.)

Although granted municipal status in 1423, Łódź is a 19th-century urban phenomenon. Widescale industrialisation launched by the government of the autonomous Kingdom of Poland (1816-1831) chose the watershed between the Vistula and the Warta, with an abundant supply of pure spring water, as an area suitable for the future textile industry. Numerous new settlements, headed by Łódź, attracted weavers from Bohemia, Saxony and Silesia. In 1835-1837, Ludwik Geyer built Poland's first steam spinning mill, an initiative emulated by other entrepreneurs. The lifting of customs barriers between the Congress Kingdom and Russia in 1850 opened up absorbent Russian markets; consequently, more and larger factories were built: spinning and weaving mills, bleacheries and dye-houses. The export of products and import of commodities were facilitated by railway lines built in the second half of the century. Łódź became the largest textile producer in Europe after Manchester. During the 1914-1918 war, local industry suffered considerable losses – machines and installations were dismantled and removed on a huge scale as part of German efforts to "deindustrialize" the town and liquidate a competitor.

Łódź.
The Poznański
Palace, interior.

Postwar Łódź recovered rapidly, although the loss of Russian buyers curbed further progress, and the oscillating market conditions during the inter-war period did not offer conditions for uninterrupted expansion. Annexed to the Third Reich in 1939, both the town and its inhabitants endured hardships and persecution. Following liberation in 1945, the industrial works – Łódź had not been destroyed – promptly restarted production. Later years brought the advancement of other branches of the industry, particularly machine-building, chemical, electrical and clothing. The town became an important cultural centre, the seat of a university and other higher schools of learning as well as scientific institutes, theatres, a philharmonic, an opera house, museums and libraries. The territorial development of Łódź initially followed the southward plans of R. Rembieliński, chairman of the voivodeship of Mazovia (1774-1841). This was the time of the delineation of the New Town, with Wolności (Freedom) Square at its centre, encompassing the town hall and a Protestant church. The town extended along the present-day Piotrowska Street. Up to this period, development followed a rational and clearcut plan, but in the later part of the 19th century it grew more spontaneous, with tenement houses, factories, workers'

dwellings and the sumptuous palaces of factory owners chaotically appearing side by side and covering ever wider areas. After 1945, work began on remodelling the town, which assumed the role of a significant cultural centre, with numerous schools of higher learning: music and medical academies, a School of Fine Arts, a Polytechnic, a University, the celebrated State Film Academy, and seminaries. (I. J. K.)

Łódź is the home of two museums unique for their highly specialised collections. The Museum of Art, while exhibiting older Polish and foreign works of art, concentrates on 20th-century avant-garde artists, including the Constructivists. The second museum, connected especially with the town's past and specific character as a textile manufacturing centre, is the Central Museum of the Textile Industry, organised in 1960 in former factory buildings from the 19th century. Apart from exhibits relating to the history of the industry, the museum collects Polish tapestries, including the particularly noteworthy kilim rugs and wall hangings from the 18th century, decorative sashes typical of Polish noble dress in the 17th and 18th century, and contemporary, experimental tapestries by leading Polish artists. (P. T.)

on the right:
Łódź.
Piotrkowska Street.

Situated at the junction of Great Poland, Little Poland and Mazovia, Piotrków Trybunalski, originally a centre of ducal landed estates, was granted municipal rights at the end of the 13th century. From the 14th to the 18th century, it played an important political role as the site of gentry assemblies, parliamentary sessions and Church synods. From 1578 to 1792, it was the seat of the Crown Tribunal. In the 17th and 18th century, the town was seriously damaged by fires and wars, and did not regain its economic and cultural importance until the 19th century. Today, Piotrków is a centre of the machine, glass and textile industries. Its numerous historical monuments include Gothic and Baroque monasteries, a castle from 1511, 18th- and 19th-century merchants' houses and the oldest landmark, namely, a Gothic parish church with Baroque chapels (first recorded in 1349). (I. J. K.)

The small town of Łęczyca in the valley of the Bzura, on the borderline between Greater Poland and Mazovia, boasts of ancient history and former splendour. The original stronghold, on the site of the present-day village of Tum, dates from the 6th-8th century. Łęczyca was the centre of the Łężyczanie tribe; included into the state of Mieszko I, it subsequently attained the rank of the seat of one of the oldest castellanships in Poland. A Benedictine abbey, established here in the 11th century, became the property of the bishops of Gniezno. In 1161, a spacious Romanesque collegiate church was consecrated on the site of the abbey. During the 13th century, Łęczyca became the capital of a duchy, and from the 14th century it assumed the functions of the capital of a voivodeship. Kazimierz the Great surrounded the town with walls and erected a castle. The most important extant monument, namely, the Romanesque defensive arch-collegiate church on Tum, originally constructed of stone, was remodelled on several occasions, and in 1939 bombed and burned. Postwar conservation, which lasted until 1961, led to the second consecration of the church. Further restoration of this exceptional object was initiated in 1991. (I. J. K.)

on the left:

Tum near Łęczyca. Collegiate church of the Holy Virgin Mary and St. Alexis (about 1140-1161).

on pages 218-219:

■ **Piotrków Trybunalski. Church of St. James.**

■ **Łęczyca. Castle built by Kazimierz the Great in the second half of the 14th century.**

THE MAZOVIA -PODLASIE LOWLAND

Warsaw, the capital and heart of Poland, lies in the very centre of the Mazovian Lowland. Traces of settlement reach back to the Palaeolithic and Bronze Age. During the 10th -11th century, the right bank of the Vistula was the site of the Old Bródno stronghold, and from the 11th century the settlements of Kamion and Solec lay on both banks. The stronghold of Jazdów developed in the 13th century on the left bank, and by the end of that century a castle-town had been erected for the local castellan. The urban settlement of Old Warsaw evolved in the vicinity of the Castle Square at the turn of the 13th century. In 1408, an agricultural-crafts settlement adjoining the main township to the north was excluded from the jurisdiction of the *wójt* (elder) of Old Warsaw and became known as the New Town (Nowe Miasto). The importance of Warsaw was greatly enhanced by the transference of the ducal seat from Czersk in 1413. The borough benefited from transit trade between the East and the West, and after 1466 mainly from the Vistula trade. Banking and the crafts developed. After Mazovia's incorporation into the Crown (1526) and the Union of Lublin (1569) Warsaw became the seat of the Diet and the site of royal elections, and in 1596 – the capital of Poland. Zygmunt III Vasa expanded and remodelled the ducal castle into a royal residence. Spatial growth was accompanied by changes in the urban structure. The Gothic town houses grouped around the Market Square of the Old Town were redesigned and enlarged in the Renaissance and Baroque style; the gentry and magnates residing in the capital founded the so-called jurisdictions, their own private townships exempt from municipal law, where they built churches and palaces. A separate town – Praga – grew up on the east bank.

on the right:

**Warsaw.
Ujazdowski Park,
laid out in 1893-1896
according to a project by
Franciszek Szanior.**

Swedish invasions of the mid-17th and early 18th century incurred serious damage and ruined the burghers. Recovery came in the second half of the 18th century, during the reign of King Stanisław August Poniatowski, a great patron of the arts, literature and education. Trade expanded, as did manufactures and banks. Merchants built new houses while magnates invested in palaces. Warsaw became a progressive centre of the Enlightenment. Political and social reform movements were reflected in the Third May Constitution, passed in 1791. Administrative order was introduced, and private townships were liquidated in order to create a single urban organism. The final, third partition of Poland degraded Warsaw to the status of a Prussian provincial seat (1796-1806), revived after it became the administrative centre of the Grand Duchy of Warsaw (1806-1815), and especially the seat of the authorities governing the autonomous Kingdom of Poland (1815-1831). Economic, political and cultural life flourished, the city expanded, and monumental Classicist structures were erected. The University was opened in 1816, the Conservatory in 1821, and the Polytechnical Institute in 1826. The Society of Friends of Science acted as a patron of academic life, and the Polski Theatre, established in 1800, played a similar role in culture. Growing political conspiracies led to the outbreak of the November Uprising of 1830-1831. After the disastrous failure of the insurrection the tsarist authorities liquidated autonomy, resorted to political terror, and closed all schools of higher learning and scientific institutions. Undaunted, cultural and academic life concentrated in the editorial offices of various periodicals, surviving scientific societies, and private salons. Theatres also continued to function. The School of Fine Arts, previously a university department, was reopened in 1844, and in 1862 the University itself returned to life as the Main School. Artistic, literary and scientific patronage gradually became the domain of the bourgeoisie, which supplanted the aristocracy and was assigned increasing prominence due to the development of the economy, which during the mid-19th century was in the throes of the Industrial Revolution.

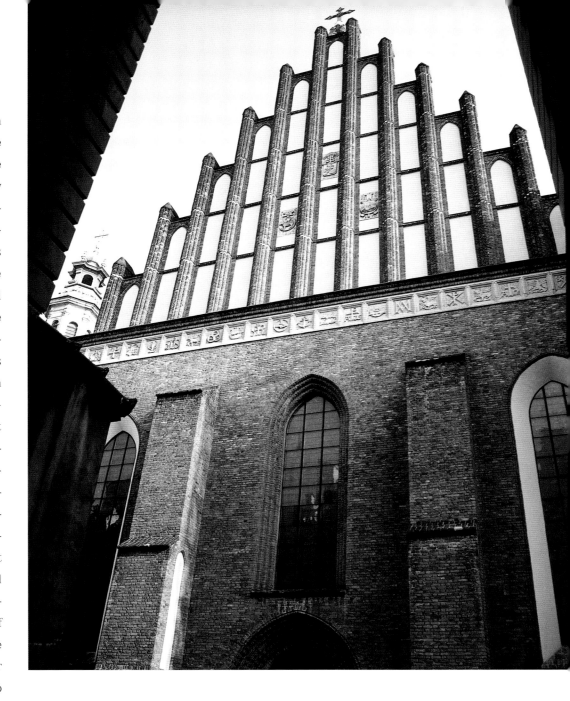

Assorted clandestine pro-independence organisations pursued their activity. During the January Uprising (1863-1864) Warsaw became the seat of the National Government. The collapse of the insurrection denoted the loss of intellectual and cultural primacy in favour of Cracow and Lvov, although Warsaw continued to be the scene of economic growth. The expansion of industry was accompanied by a rise of the working class. The revolution of 1905-1907 succeeded in winning the legalisation of Polish private schools and the right to organise scientific, artistic and social societies.

In 1918, Warsaw became the capital of an independent Polish state and the focal point of political, cultural and academic life. This was the time of spatial expansion as well as assorted urban-planning and

Warsaw. Arch-cathedral of the Decapitation of St. John the Baptist.

on the left:
Warsaw. View of the tower of the church of St. Martin.

on pages 224-225:
Warsaw. Old Town Market Square, the Kołłątaj (western) side

communal undertakings. The population of Warsaw, Poland's main Resistance centre during the second world war, suffered enormous losses totalling about 800 000 persons (killed and deported). Monuments of national culture, works of art, book collections, archives and museums were destroyed or plundered. Some 85% of left-bank Warsaw, where the Uprising of 1944 took place, was razed. Contrary to all odds, postwar Warsaw remained the capital of the country, rebuilt thanks to the joint effort of the whole of Polish society. Ultimately, the town was reconstructed and expanded on a considerably enlarged area. The historical monuments of Warsaw suffered from particularly severe destruction, primarily as a result of the policy of intentional devastation implemented by the Nazi authorities. The reconstruction programme restored the highly valued monuments and historic urban plan, such as the Old Town with its mediaeval walls, the New Town, and the Teatralny, Bankowy and Zamkowy squares (a Gothic bridge leading to the Old Town was unearthed underneath the latter). The Royal Castle was rebuilt with the active cooperation of Polish society and Polish communities living abroad; the reconstruction embraced the interiors, with attempts at restoring their original appearance by using extant and salvaged elements of the castle. (I. J. K.)

In the second half of the 17th century, the principal architect in Warsaw and Poland was Tylman van Gameren, a Dutchman brought to Poland from Utrecht by Stanisław Herakliusz Lubomirski in

Warsaw. View of the Royal Castle with a bridge of the former Krakowska Gate.

on the left:

Warsaw. Royal Castle, Old Audience Hall, 1775-1777, design: Domenico Merlini.

Warsaw. The Krasiński (Commonwealth) Palace in Krasińskich Square, built in the second half of the 17th century, designed by Tylman van Gameren.

around 1666, and six years later ennobled as Tylman Gamerski. Although he had been educated as a painter, Gameren was the author of excellent architectural plans; he was trained in Venice but his works took on a true northern character. One of Gameren's masterpieces realised in Warsaw is the Krasiński Palace, erected in 1677-1682 and completed by 1697, a supreme example of European Baroque architecture. The interiors, featuring an imposing staircase, excellent proportions of the whole edifice and each detail, and the superb sculpted decoration by Andreas Schlüter of Gdańsk, an

artist who later became widely reputed throughout Europe, comprise a perfect, harmonious entity. Another important example of Tylman van Gameren's oeuvre is the church of St. Boniface (1687-1692) in the district of Czerniaków, a rural building combining a modest exterior with exceptionally rich interiors in which the architect succeeded in achieving an effect of monumentality by applying suitable proportions. Frescoes, stucco and gilding do not obliterate architectural forms, and all domains of the arts, including music and unusual light effects, achieve harmony concurrent with the

aesthetic principles of the mature Baroque.

The early 19th-century architect Antonio Corazzi played a role in the history of Warsaw similar to Tylman van Gameren during the late 17th century. The Italian architect, brought to Poland from Livorno by Stanisław Staszic, worked in Warsaw for more than a quarter of a century. Although lacking the exceptional talents of his Dutch predecessor, Corazzi, a representative of an academic version of Classicism, was indubitably a talented town planner. He successfully closed off Krakowskie Przedmieście Street with his design of a building intended for the War-

saw Friends of Science, proposed an interesting solution for Bankowy Square by lining it with a row of public buildings for the government of the Duchy of Warsaw, and endowed a former market place with monumental proportions by means of the elongated façade of the Wielki (Grand) Theatre, erected in 1825-1833. At the time of its completion, this was the most modern theatre building in Europe, whose scale surpassed similar objects. (P. T.)

The most beautiful façade of all Warsaw churches belongs to the Visitant church in Krakowskie Przed-

Warsaw. The Staszic Palace, designed by Antonio Corazzi from 1820-1823.

mieście Street. Although raised in two stages in 1727-1734 and 1754-1763, and therefore between the Late Baroque and the Rococo, this design remains exceptionally uniform. Columns and cornices dominate the façade, below which the walls seem to undulate. The monumental façade is, at the same time, extremely detailed and defined by chiaroscuro effects. The Rococo interiors are equally harmonious. Despite the excellence of the building the name of its architect name remains unknown; it has been suggested that he could have been Karol Bay or Giacomo Fontana. The statue of Cardinal Stefan Wyszyński unveiled in front of the church in 1986 was executed by Andrzej Renes. (P. T.)

Important events in the history of Poland are associated with the Koniecpolski-Radziwiłł Palace, built in the mid-17th century and expanded in the following century. The present-day façade dates from 1819 and was designed by Christian Piotr Aigner. A statue of Prince Józef Poniatowski stands in front of the palace since 1965. This monument to the leader of the Polish forces during the Napoleonic wars had a truly dramatic history, perhaps more than any other statue in Warsaw, before it was blown up by the Germans in 1944. Since it was an original work of the famous Danish sculptor Bertel Thorvaldsen, who executed it in 1829-1832, it was replaced by a copy presented to the city by the people of Copenhagen. A mark of the destruction incurred upon Warsaw by the Nazi occupant is the Tomb of the Unknown Soldier, a fragment of the monumental Neoclassical colonnade of the Saski (Saxon) Palace, blown up by the Germans. (P. T.)

The Classicist Staszic Palace in Nowy Świat Street was built in 1820-1823 according to a design by Antonio Corazzi and upon the initiative of Stanisław Staszic, as the seat of the Society of Friends of Science. A statue of Copernicus, another work by Thorvaldsen, was placed in front of the building in 1830. After the January Uprising of 1863-1864 the palace was remodelled by the tsarist authorities for the purposes of a Russian secondary school, which entailed changing the elevation and the addition of an Ortho-

on the right:
Warsaw.
The Presidential Palace
in Krakowskie
Przedmieście Street,
designed by Christian
Piotr Aigner.

dox chapel in the Neo-Byzantine style. The Classicist forms were reinstated in 1924-1926, but the original Corazzi façade, burnt during the Warsaw Uprising of 1944, was not recreated until 1947-1950.

The predecessor of the Ostrogski Palace, also known as the Gniński or Ordynacki Palace, on Tamka Street, was a fortified castle whose lower walls originate from the turn of the 16th century. The building was begun in 1609 by Janusz Ostrogski, and completed by the Gniński family upon the basis of a design by Tylman van Gameren. Redesigned upon numerous occasions, the palace, almost totally ruined in 1944, was reconstructed and regained its façade from the end of the 17th century. The building often changed owners and users, and today houses the Frederic Chopin Society.

The church of St. Alexander standing in the middle of Trzech Krzyży (Three Crosses) Square, a Classicist copy of the Pantheon in Rome (P. Aigner, 1818-1825), was reconstructed in 1886-1894, destroyed in 1944, and rebuilt in its original form after the war. The restored Royal Road (Trakt Królewski) stretches from the Royal Castle southwards, to the Belweder (Belvedere) Palace, situated at the edge of the Łazienki Park. Originally, the park was the hunting ground of the Mazovian dukes. An early 17th-century bath house, built in the middle of a pond, was expanded in the second half of the century by Tylman van Gameren for Stanisław Herakliusz Lubomirski and lent its name to the park and palace complex. The Baroque pavilion housing the baths was situated on an island surrounded by canals. In 1764, Łazienki was acquired by King Stanisław Augustus Poniatowski. Avenues were laid out among the forested terrain, the canals next to the palace were transformed into ponds, and new buildings were erected. From 1775, the bath pavilion was gradually adapted for the purposes of a royal residence, known from then on as the Łazienki Palace, the Palace on the Island or the Palace on the Water, enlarged thanks to new, elaborately decorated interiors. Two pavilions connected with the main building by means of bridges with colonnades were added. The construction work, supervised by the

King, was realised by a group of artists: architects Domenico Merlini and Jan Chrystian Kamsetzer and interior designers Jan Bogumil Plersch, Marceli Bacciarelli, André Le Brun and Franciszek Pinck. The Myślewicki Palace and the Little White House were erected in the park in 1774-1776. The Trou Madame pavilion, built near the main Łazienki Palace, was soon transformed into the Little Theatre. The Amphitheatre on the Water was constructed on the bank of the southern pond, and a guardhouse overlooked the northern pond; the existing outbuilding was enlarged. The Orangery, whose eastern wing housed yet another theatre, was constructed at the foot of the escarpment. The park was designed in the English style by Jan Christian Schuch, and enhanced with bowers, small bridges and sculptures. The view to the south ended on a cascade, while that to the north looked on to a statue of King Jan III Sobieski. The King and his court resided in Łazienki during

Warsaw. Church of St. Alexander in Trzech Krzyży Square, designed by Christian Piotr Aigner.

on the left:

Warsaw. The Ostrogski Palace in Tamka Street.

on pages 234-235:

Warsaw. Palace on the Water in Łazienki Park, northern façade.

Warsaw.
Theatre on the Island
in Łazienki Park.

the summer months. Colourful spectacles were held in the park, theatrical performances were staged, and the cultural and intellectual elite gathered for the famous Thursday dinners at the Palace. In 1817, Łazienki passed into the hands of Tsar Alexander I. New utilitarian buildings were put up in 1819-1839, the Trou Madame pavilion was redesigned into the New Guardroom, and the Great Outbuilding became the seat of the Cadets School. The Łazienki Palace and Park complex remained virtually unchanged until 1939. At the beginning of the war, part of the palace outfitting was transferred to the National Museum. Following the collapse of the Warsaw Uprising, the palace interior was set on fire; the Nazis prepared to dynamite the building and it was only a lucky coincidence that it escaped complete

destruction. Reconstruction began immediately after liberation. Museums were arranged in the Palace on the Water, the theatre in the Orangery and the Little White House. The freestanding sculptures and the statue of Frederic Chopin by Wacław Szymanowski, unveiled in 1926, were also restored. Noontime Chopin concerts are held at the foot of the statue every Sunday during the spring and summer season. The Belvedere complex above the Vistula escarpment is connected with the Łazienki Palace and Park. The original villa, probably wooden, was raised in 1659 for Krzysztof Pac, the Grand Chancellor of Lithuania, and named Belvedere due to the beautiful site and vista (Italian: bel vedere). The successive owners, the Lubomirski family, built a new, Baroque palace (1730-1750), which after 1767 belonged to

the King, and following his death – to his brother, Prince Józef Poniatowski. Brought in 1818 by the government of the Kingdom of Poland from the Kicki family, the Belvedere became the residence of the Tsar's brother, the Grand Prince Constantine. Between 1818 and 1822, the palace was designed in the Neoclassical style, with a four-column portico facing the courtyard and garden, and ground-floor wings enclosing the courtyard. A landscape garden was created at the foot of the escarpment. Since 1918, the Belvedere has been the official state residence of the President of Poland. (I. J. K.)

When in 1674 Jan Sobieski ascended the Polish throne, he embarked upon building a suburban residence at Wilanów (at the time still known as Milanów). The original ground-floor manor house with alcoves, typical of the time, was rapidly extended (1681-1682), probably by Tylman van Gameren. The final phase in the expansion of Wilanów during the King's lifetime look place in 1684-1696 under the guidance of Augustyn Locci, a Polonised Italian. The resultant extensive complex was composed of a main building, galleries topped with towers, and palace wings on either side of the courtyard. Reputed artists, including the Gdańsk sculptors Andreas Schluter and Stefan Szwaner, the stucco decorator Giuseppe Belotti, the acclaimed fresco painter Michelangelo Palloni, the Frenchman Claude Callot, and two Poles, Jerzy Eleuter Szymonowicz-Siemiginowski and Jan Reisner, both educated in Italy at the King's expense, worked with Locci. The façades disclose all the characteristic features of the Late Baroque, and

Warsaw. Palace in Wilanów from the approach.

on page 239:

Warsaw. Palace of Culture and Science in Defilady Square, view from the Congress Hall.

blend together architecture, sculpture and paintings, producing the effect of opulence and picturesqueness. A parade courtyard was laid out on the palace's axis, and a geometrical French garden – in back of the residence. The successive owners of Wilanów continued expanding and remodelling the original palace and its surrounding until the beginning of the 20th century. Today, the Wilanów complex is composed of about seventy palatial interiors typical for the 17th, 18th and 19th century. Fragments from the reign of Jan II Sobieski are the most valuable in view of the fact that they are the only authentic Baroque residential interiors in Poland. The palace's devastation under the Nazi occupation necessitated painstaking restoration and suitable exposition. In the spirit of Sarmatian ideology the impressive façade decorations and the interiors of the palace refer to Roman antiquity and extol the virtues and deeds of the king and the charm of his wife. In contrast to most Baroque residences of this sort, the state rooms are located on the ground floor, thus reflecting the absence of a striving towards emphasis on monumentality and power, a trait typical of royal residences. The avoidance of grandiose forms and stress placed on horizontal rather than vertical forms enabled Wilanów Palace to retain privacy and a non-regal scale. Apart from the period interiors, the palace houses a gallery of Polish portraits from the 16th to the 19th century; the for-

mer orangery features an exhibition of the arts and crafts. In 1968, the building of the former riding school was adapted into a Poster Museum. (P. T.)

During the 19th century, the centre of Warsaw shifted westwards, to the area along Marszałkowska Street and the perpendicularly intersecting Jerozolimskie Avenue. Postwar reconstruction considerably broadened the main streets; Marszałkowska Street in particular took on a new appearance due to the erection of public buildings, shops and residential houses. The sprawling Defilady Square on the western side of the street became dominated by the commanding Palace of Culture and Science, built in 1952-1955, a monumental,

Warsaw. Siekierkowski Bridge.

pseudo-Classical skyscraper, at the time described as a gift from the people of the Soviet Union. The palace, modelled on Moscow buildings of the Stalinist era, housed the Polish Academy of Sciences, numerous scientific societies, several theatres and cinemas, exhibition and sports halls, and a number of restaurants. The Congress Hall seats 3 200 people. In 1960-1969, a complex of three-storey department stores (today: the Centrum Gallery) was built on the opposite side of Marszałkowska Street. Behind them stretches "Pasaż Śródmiejski" (The City Passage), intended excessively for pedestrians. Lofty residential housing appeared in the background of the main thoroughfare.

The Central Railway Station was built in 1972-1976 some distance to the west from the intersec-

tion of Marszałkowska Street and Jerozolimskie Avenue. Opposite stands the Marriott Hotel, completed in 1989. The skyscrapers erected in the City during the 1990s include the Warsaw Financial Centre, the FIM Tower with a characteristic orange lattice comprising the lower half of the building, and the Reform Plaza. The panorama of the Wola district is dominated by the Daewoo offices – the towering Warsaw Trade Centre. (I. J. K.)

Among the more than forty assorted museums in Warsaw, the most important is the National Museum, founded in 1862 as a Museum of Fine Arts. Its collections encompass all periods, from antiquity to modern times, and embrace numerous cultures.

The ancient art gallery displays works acquired in the course of excavations conducted by Polish specialists in Egypt, Syria, Sudan and Cyprus. Particularly notable are the 71 Coptic-Byzantine paintings from the cathedral at Faras in Sudan. The gallery of mediaeval art contains works of art from various parts of Poland, spanning from the early 13th century to the mid-16th century, the largest Polish collection outside Cracow. Particularly noteworthy exhibits are examples of the Warsaw realist school from the late 19th century. The most interesting part of the collection of modern foreign art represents North European schools – the Low Countries, Germany and 17th-century Netherlands. A great number of impressive works of art is to be found in the reconstructed chambers of the Royal Castle. Polish art is exemplified by portraits of monarchs and historic personages from the time of Stanisław Augustus Poniatowski. The Castle showrooms exhibit paintings and sculptures of assorted European schools as well as objects of the decorative crafts, used to outfit the period interiors.

A number of new monuments has been unveiled in Warsaw during the past few years: a statue of Marshal Józef Piłsudski in Piłsudski Square, executed by Tadeusz Łodziany (1995), a monument commemorating "Those Who Fallen and Were Killed in the East" in Muranowska Street, designed by Maksymilian Biskupski (1995), and a state of Henryk Sienkiewcz in the Łazienki Park, executed by Gustaw Zemła (2000).

Warsaw.
The Metropolitan
office building in
Piłsudskiego Square,
design: Norman
Foster.

on pages 242-243:

Mazovian landscape.

The town of Płock, strikingly situated on the high bank of the Vistula, is the oldest settlement in Mazovia. In the 8th-9th century it was the centre of a pagan cult, and by the 10th century – a ducal stronghold. During the 11th century, Płock was the seat of a castellanship and, subsequently, of a bishopric. The 12th-century castle-town became the capital of the province of Mazovia, and then the centre of the duchy of Płock. The year 1237 marked the establishment of a self-governing municipal commune. The reign of Kazimierz the Great witnessed the erection of a new castle, and the town was encircled with defence walls. Płock flourished thanks to the Vistula trade and well-developed crafts. Prosperity favoured the advancement of culture and the arts. During the 17th and

18th century, wars, conflagrations and pestilence hampered growth until the Enlightenment. The brief period of affiliation to Prussia (1793-1806) altered the urban layout: part of the castle and the defence walls were pulled down, and a New Town was built in the suburbs. Economic, cultural and intellectual life revived in the 19th century. Incorporated into the German Reich in 1939, Płock became an important centre of the Resistance movement; its population suffered large wartime losses. Dynamic development since 1945 was due primarily to a huge petrochemical plant built in the 1960s. Płock was rapidly transformed into a major industrial centre with engineering works, food processing factories, timber plants, and textile enterprises. It is also an important river port with the

Płock.
Classicist town hall designed by Jakub Kubicki, built in 1824-1827.

on the left:
Płock.
View of cathedral hill from the Vistula.

The town of Ciechanów lies in the valley of the Łydynia to the north-east of Płock. The Gothic brick castle of the Mazovian dukes was constructed in ca. 1429 on a rectangular plan with two circular corner towers. A two-storey residential building was erected in the courtyard. From 1526, the castle belonged to Queen Bona, the wife of Zygmunt the Old. The castle started to decline in the wake of the Swedish wars, and at the end of the 18th century the residential part was pulled down by the Prussian authorities. Ciechanów Castle is an example of a regular, lowland fortress. Reconstructed, it now houses the Regional Museum in Ciechanów. (P.T.)

An original example of the Romantic return to mediaeval art is the small castle at Opinogóra, built by General Wincenty Krasiński; some researchers maintain that the plans were drawn up in the first half of the 19th century by the famous French architect and conservator Eugène-Emanuel Viollet-le-Duc. The postwar castle interiors were suitably arranged so as to display exhibits associated with Zygmunt Krasiński, the outstanding Polish Romantic poet. The castle forms part of a larger complex consisting of a church with the poet's tomb, a cemetery and a beautiful landscape park. (P.T.)

Already in the 13th century Pułtusk on the Narew, situated beyond the Zegrzyński Estuary, was known as a castellanship town belonging to the bishops of Płock. It received municipal rights twice: in 1257 and then in 1339, after it was burned down by the Lithuanian army. Rapid growth took place from the 15th to the 17th century, when Pułtusk was one of the main economic centres of the region. Trade in agricultural products and timber was favoured by the town's advantageous location on the river which served as the main transportation route to Gdańsk. Special attention is due to the Gothic collegiate church of the Holy Virgin Mary, constructed around 1443 with Renaissance interiors and a bishops' sepulchral chapel. A lofty Classicist bell tower from the end of the 18th century can be seen from afar. In 1944, more than 70% of Pułtusk lay in ruins. Today, the town is a celebrated academic centre (the Humanities Academy).

Pułtusk.
Market Square.

Pułtusk.
Castle of the bishops
of Płock, today:
the Polonia House.

on the right;

Opinogóra.
Neo-Gothic castle of
the Krasiński family,
today: Museum of
Romanticism.

largest river shipyard in Poland. The town has remained an important cultural and academic centre. Its numerous museums and historical monuments include the unique Płock Doors made of bronze in Madgeburg in the middle of the 12th century for Płock cathedral. The quarters of the doors, which already during the Middle Ages were used for the St. Sophie cathedral in Novgorod, depict scenes from the life of Christ and the Old Testament as well as a symbolic battle waged between virtues and vices. On 23 November 1981, more than 500 years later, a bronze copy of the original doors was installed in Płock cathedral. The Museum of Mazovia feature archaeological, historical and ethnographic exhibits, as well as a particularly interesting Art Nouveau collection. (I. J. K.)

Sierpc. ▪▫
Skansen museum
of the Mazovian
village.

Brochów. ▪▫
Fortified basilica
of St. Roch.

The forest, dune and marsh complex of Kampinos Forest occupies the Central Mazovian Lowland and stretches as far as the north-western limits of Warsaw. Natural resources and landscape merits were decisive for the establishment of the Kampinos National Park (1959), encompassing nine strict reserves. Two belts of sand dunes rise above the swampy lowlands. Pine woods predominate, followed by mixed forest, oak and hornbeam woods, alders, peatbogs, meadows and sand grasses. Quicksand appears in spots devoid of vegetation. Kampinos Forest, which originally belonged to the Mazovian dukes and later to the Polish monarchs, became a popular hunting ground once the capital of Poland had been transferred to Warsaw. The mediaeval forest was inhabited by European bisons, anrochs and bears. The scare monuments of nature which had sur-

vived to our time are the only traces of the primeval woods. The animal world is represented by species common in the Lowland, and only the elk, extinct already at the beginning of the 19th century, was reintroduced after 1945. Today, intense efforts are made to reinstate the original flora and fauna. Countless crosses, graves and cemeteries testify to the battles waged in Kampinos Forest across the ages. In 1939, divisions of the Polish army retreated through the Forest towards the besieged capital. During the occupation, Kampinos was the site of battles conducted by partisan units. In 1939-1945, the Germans shot thousands of Poles in a wood near the village of Palmiry, including outstanding representatives of political, academic and cultural life. A cemetery-monument commemorating the victims of Nazi crimes was created here in 1948. (I. J. K.)

The village of Brochów on the edge of Kampinos Forest was founded by the dukes of 12th-century Mazovia. Today, it features a preserved Renaissance fortified basilica with three circular towers from 1554-1561, surrounded with a 17th-century defence wall and bastions. The parents of Frederic Chopin were married here, and the composer was christened in the same church. He was born on 1 March 1810 in Żelazowa Wola, in a small manor house, a former outbuilding of the palatial residence of the Skarbek family, where he spent the first years of his life. In 1931, a museum devoted to the composer was opened in the manor house. In the summer season, outstanding pianists give Sunday concerts of Chopin's music. A statue of Chopin, unveiled in 1894, stands in the western part of the landscape park surrounding the manor house, full of interesting trees and flowers. (I. J. K.)

The fertile region of Łowicz belonged to the bishops of Gniezno as far back as the 12th century; from the 15th century, its owners were the primates of Poland who ruled it as a sovereign duchy. The principal town of Łowicz was one of the oldest castle-towns in Piast Poland. Before passing into the hands of the archbishops, Łowicz was the property of the Mazovian dukes and a castellanship seat, granted municipal rights in 1298. During the 14th century and 15th century, it developed into a large administrative and economic centre of the Church estates. Trade and crafts flourished, especially cloth and tile production. In the 15th century, the fortified castle, originally built at the turn of the 14th century, became an impressive residence of the Primate of Poland. Powerful fortifications were put up in 1655 after Łowicz was captured by the Swedes. Subsequently, the withdrawing invaders destroyed the cas-

Żelazowa Wola. Manor house – the birthplace of Frederic Chopin.

on pages 250-251:

Ruins of Ciechanów Castle – one of the largest mediaeval fortresses in Mazovia.

tle buildings and the borough. Incorporated by Prussia in 1795, the town of Łowicz, together with the landed estates, which from the 17th century were known as the Duchy of Łowicz, became government property. In 1807, Napoleon I conferred the duchy to Marshal L. N. Davout, and in 1820 Tsar Alexander I granted it to his brother, Prince Constantine; hence the title of Duchess of Łowicz assumed by Joanna Grudzińska, Constantine's wife and co-owner of the estates. In 1829, the Duchy was enlarged after the addition of Skierniewice and several landed estates. During the 1820s, it became the scene of the first, exemplary introduction of ground rent to the local peasants. The already possessed and newly obtained freedoms, fertile soil, and relatively large farms contributed to the prosperity of the peasants, who became known as Księżaki; the same assets favoured the development of folk culture. After 1838, the Duchy was ruled directly by the tsars, who transferred its administrative centre to Skierniewice where they had a residence. At the time, Łowicz was an important market and crafts centre, although the impact of the wool and farm produce fairs held here was wider. Badly damaged in 1939, the town was rebuilt and today continues to provide services to the local farmers; farm-food, textile, metallurgical, wood and folk-art industries prevail. The town also acts as the sightseeing focal point of a region with well-preserved traditions of folk culture and an active Society of Friends of the Town and Region of Łowicz; the Łowicz Museum features numerous examples of still vigorous folk art and material culture. The colourful peasant costumes, part of the retained folk tradition and way of life, may be admired in their full beauty during the annual Corpus Christi procession. Other unique qualities of the Łowicz region are reflected in local folk music and songs, carved figures of saints in roadside shrines, and cottages, decorated both outside and inside and containing equally gaily embellished furnishing and utensils. (I. J. K.)

Nieborów and the nearby Romantic park of Arkadia lie between Łowicz and Skierniewice, on the edge of Bolimowska Forest. In 1690-1696, Tylman van

Gameren, the great Polish Baroque architect, designed the palace at Nieborów for Primate Michał Radziejowski and planned the geometric French gardens. In the following century, the palace interiors were refashioned and a complex of outbuildings was added. Nieborów maiolica was manufactured from 1881 to 1914; the residence contains numerous examples of the characteristically decorated ceramic. In spite of later changes, Nieborów is the relatively best preserved illustration of a 17th-- 18th-century palace complex with authentic 18th-- and 19th-century interiors featuring Polish and English furniture, Oriental tapestries, Wedgewood and Sèvres porcelain, numerous portraits and a rich collection of old prints in the library. Two Venetian globes, executed by Vincenzo Coronelli in the late 17th century and originally displayed at Versailles, are well worth the visitor's attention. Fragments of classical statues,

Region of Łowicz.
Folk costumes.

on the left:
Łowicz. Cathedral.

tombstones, sarcophagi and urns testify to a Romantic fascination with the past. A typically Baroque geometric park is preserved along the axis of the palace, and a landscape park was laid out in the mid-18th century. (P. T.)

The most interesting Romantic park in Poland can be found at Arkadia, a few kilometres from Nieborów. Planned in 1778 by the architect Szymon Bogumił Zug at the request of Helena Radziwiłł (the co-author of the design), it was not completed until 1821. The park complies with English models and represents a combination of freely evolving plants and buildings from different epochs and styles, some of which were intentionally designed as ancient ruins. The central architectural element is the Neoclassical Temple of Diana. The walls of the High Priest's House incorporate numerous fragments of historic

buildings, and the Gothic House was designed exceptionally by the painter Alexander Orłowski. Other structures include an Aqueduct, a Greek Arch, and the Grotto of Sybil. The designers resigned from opening up endless perspectives and avoided dominant spatial accents in order to produce the impression of unhampered picturesqueness. Retaining almost all of its original elements, Arkadia best reflects the manner in which the Romantic call for a return to nature was implemented. (P. T.)

To the west of Łowicz lies Walewice, whose landmark is the Classicist palace, the residence of Maria Walewska, Napoleon's famous Polish lover, built in 1783. Today, the palace houses the offices of a stud farm celebrated for breeding Arab horses and holding a national championship: the Comprehensive Saddle Horse Competition (WKKW).

The town of Czersk, located along the southern edge of the Warsaw agglomeration, was a castle-town during the 11th century, the seat of a castellanship, and in 1262-1429 the capital of the duchy of Mazovia, enjoying municipal status since 1350. It became known for its cloth and beer, and traded in grain and timber. The transference of the ducal residence to Warsaw and a shift in the course of the Vistula hampered further development, while the Swedish invasions led to decline. Today, the inhabitants of Czersk are mainly engaged in fruit and vegetable growing. The ruins of the Gothic castle of the Mazovian dukes built at the beginning of the 15th century, with two circular turrets from the 15th and 16th century and a gate tower preceded by a bridge from the mid-16th century, overlook the town. Archaeological research conducted near the castle ruins since 1965 has revealed the existence of a timber-earth defensive stronghold, burned down at the end of the 12th century and later transformed into a cemetery. (I. J. K.)

Pilica, a left-bank tributary of the Vistula, is one of the most beautiful rivers of the Polish Lowland. Its source is situated on the Cracow-Częstochowa Upland, and the lower course flows through a broad valley whose northern verge offers an extensive view over the valley meadows and pasturelands as well as the more distant, dense forests. (I. J. K.)

Sulejów, lying on both banks of the Pilica, is a centre for the surrounding rural Piotrków Plain; a town with little industry, it is chiefly a summer and tourist resort. The nearby woods and the Sulejów artificial lake to the north of the town create excellent conditions for recreation. The town was built next to a ford across the Pilica, and already in the first half of the 12th century it included a customs house. In 1176-1177, Kazimierz the Just founded a fortified Cistercian abbey on the right bank, closed during the cassation of the order in 1819. The Late Romanesque stone basilica with a transept, erected before 1232, has been partly reconstructed. The preserved fragments of the abbey include the eastern

on the left:

Walewice.
Classical palace
from 1783, built
according to a project
by Hilary Szpilowski.

on pages 258-259:

Czersk.
Castle ruins.

Puławy.
Landscape park, the
Temple of Sybil.

Sulejów.
Late Romanesque
church of the Cistercian
abbey – the basilica of
St. Thomas.

on the right:
Sulejów.
Main portal of the
basilica of St. Thomas.

on pages 262-263:
Puławy.
The Czartoryski Palace.

wing of a late-Romanesque chapel house, Gothic cloisters from the early 15th century, fortifications with gates and towers, and an arsenal. The main body of the abbey houses a regional museum, with collections illustrating the history of the town and region of Sulejów. (I. J. K.)

The park and palace in Puławy, situated on the high right bank of the Vistula in the voivodeship of Lublin, played an important role in Polish history and culture at the end of the 18th century. The aristocratic residence of the Czartoryski family attracted Enlightenment-era artists, poets and scholars, thus competing with the Warsaw milieu of King Stanisław Augustus Poniatowski. One of the intentions of this monarch was to set up Musaeum Polonicum, which would gather works of art and historic souvenirs. The royal plans were successfully executed by the Czartoryskis of Puławy. After 1800, the architect Christian Piotr Aigner built in the park a Gothic House and the Temple of Sybil, modelled on the ancient Roman edifice. A collection of paintings displayed in the Gothic House, including masterpieces by Raphael, Leonardo da Vinci and Rembrandt, became the basis of the Czartoryski Museum in Cracow. The Temple of Sybil, which accommodated mementos of Copernicus, Żółkiewski and Kościuszko as well as royal insignia and banners, was the first

**Radzyń Podlaski.
Palace.**

national museum in Poland, envisaged as a fount of patriotic hope during the partition era. At present, the palace is the seat of the Institute of Land Cultivation, Fertilisation and Soil Science. (P. T.)

The small town of Radzyń Podlaski to the north-east of Puławy has preserved two valuable monuments of architecture. The church from 1641 is a typical example of Polish Mannerism; its slender body with buttresses and narrow windows refers to Gothic forms, a frequent tendency in Mannerist art. The interiors feature characteristic stuccoed vaulting and

a Mannerist tombstone of the Mniszech family. The second object is a palace from the end of the 17th century, initially erected for the Szczuka family by August Wincenty Locci, the co-author of Wilanów. The present shape, restored after a fire in 1944, reflects the remodelling devised by Giacomo Fontana, a renowned mid-18th century Warsaw architect, for Marshal Eustachy Potocki. The sophisticated Rococo architecture emulates superior French models and is the best example of this style in Poland. The partially preserved splendid Rococo staircase was copied in other Polish residences of the period. (P. T.)

The western part of Polesie, a sprawling East European plain, cuts into Poland *via* the central Bug, between the Krzna and Wełnianka rivers. This is Lublin Polesie, a plain dotted with numerous peat-bogs. The lakes in the southern part of the region are, as a rule, small, shallow and with overgrown banks; sometimes, they are surrounded by quagmires, which render them inaccessible.

The Bug leaves the Polesie region to the north of the mouth of the Krzna, to cut a deep valley through higher land. The steep bank near the town of Drohiczyn offers an extensive view of the meandering river valley and its left bank, which in the 13th and 14th century became the object of battles waged by Mazovia with the Lithuanians. After the Union of Lublin (1569), the region was incorporated into the Polish Kingdom. The origins of Drohiczyn can be traced back to the times of the Ruthenian settlement movement. In the 12th century, the town was the capital of the duchy of Drohiczyn. At the beginning of the early 13th century, it belonged to Duke Konrad of Mazovia, who in 1237 brought over the Knights of Christ, known as the Dobrzyń Brethren, subsequently banished by Daniel Romanovich, the Prince of Volhynia and Halicz Ukraine. Captured by the Lithuanians in 1280, Drohiczyn remained in their hands for almost 300 years; after its incorporation into the Crown, it became the capital of the voivodeship of Podlasie. Clashes during the 17th and 18th century resulted in the town's decay, furthered during both world wars. Today, this small handicrafts, trade and agricultural centre boasts of assorted vestiges of its past: a 17th-century Franciscan monastery complex, a Baroque convent and church of the Benedictine nuns from the 18th century, a Jesuit church and college from the turn of the 17th century, an Orthodox church built in the late 18th century, and a number of historic houses and manors. (I. J. K.)

At the south-eastern edge of the Podlasie Landscape Park lies Janów Podlaski, with a famous stud farm established in 1871. The first brick stables were

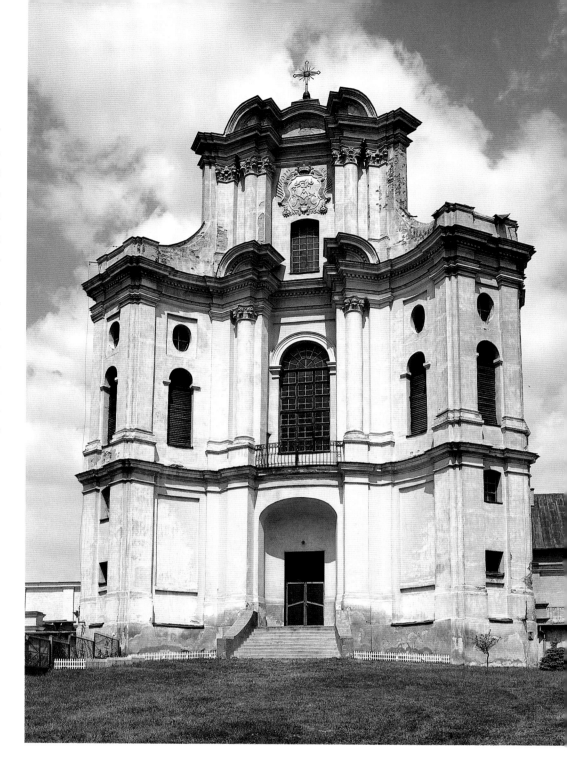

designed by Henryk Marconi. Originally, the farm bred Anglo-Arab horses, and after the first world war – thoroughbred Arab horses. Every year, the Arab Horse Days, an exceptional event held in the first half of August, include shows and an auction. Liw, some 80 km to the east of Warsaw, was the castle-town of the local castellans. The initially wooden castle, built by the Mazovian dukes, was replaced by a brick edifice (turn of the 14th century). In 1350, the trading settlement of Stary (Old) Liw, which developed at the foot of the castle, was granted municipal rights. In 1446, a second centre, which

Drohiczyn. Late Baroque church of the Benedictine nuns.

**Łomża.
Cathedral of the
Archangel Michael.**

became known as Nowy (New) Liw, was established upon the basis of a *locatio* privilege. Both centres prospered from the grain trade, and both suffered during the wars of the 17th and 18th century. United into a single urban organism in 1789, they failed to recover their former position, and in 1869 lost their urban status. Today, Liw is a small market centre and a well-known resort which derives its popularity from the River Liwiec flowing down a valley near castle hill. Wide sandy banks together with shallow and still pure water have enhanced its recreational attraction, especially for children. (I. J. K.)

At one time, the Narew, the chief river of the Podlasie region, and its tributary, the Biebrza, constituted the only route through the dense, impenetrable forests, along which the population of Mazovia made its way to Podlasie and Pruthenia. The Biebrza National Park, the largest and best preserved European complex of peatbogs with clusters of characteristic plants and the largest refuge of the elk in Poland, has been functioning since 1993. The natural ecosystem of the Biebrza Marshes is acknowledged to be one of the most unspoiled in Europe.

on the right:

**Mazovian landscape.
The river Bug.**

**Janów Podlaski.
Annual auction of
Arab horses.**

Kurpie Forest is a vestige of the once vast woodlands in the basin of the Narew in the Kurpie Lowland. Primeval vegetation has survived in several
reservations. The Narew divides the Forest into the
Zielona (Green, northern) Forest and Biała (White,
southern) Forest. Kurpie Forest was the property of
the dukes of Mazovia and then of the Polish kings.
Its inhabitants, the Kurpie people, are probably the
descendants of Mazovian settlers who during the
Middle Ages sought refuge from the Sudovians,
Lithuanians and Ruthenians. Later on, they included peasants who had fled from their masters, and

who in time were followed by members of gentry
families, fugitives from the law. Their main occupa-
tions were hunting, fishing, pitch-making, burning
charcoal, distilling potash, extracting and tooling
amber and especially wild beekeeping, pursued
until the middle of the 19th century. As the direct
subjects of the monarch, exempt from corvée, they
governed themselves by observing the beekeepers'
common law, which was not recorded until 1559,
and were ruled by their own *sołtys* (scultetus). Isolated from the outside world, the Kurpie people
retained regional distinctness, reflected in present-

day customs, architecture and costumes. Old wooden cottages, whose gables face the village road, are topped with thatched roofs. The elaborate folk costumes can be admired on religious holidays, especially Corpus Christi. Kurpie cutouts, embroidery, characteristically patterned fabrics and pottery are widely known. (I. J. K.)

Economic progress signified the relegation of traditional rural architecture in favour of new, increasingly uniform methods of construction, usually brick. The purpose of Skansen-type open-air museums in Poland is to protect relics of wooden buildings from total annihilation. The vast collections of the Museum of Farming, opened in 1963 in a restored historic palace complex in Ciechanowiec, recreate the history of agriculture in north-eastern Poland. Assorted examples of wooden rural architecture, including two arcaded manorial granaries, typical of the eastern Białystok region, a hunting lodge, seven cottages, a blacksmith's forge and water-- and windmills, have been transferred to the open-air part of the museum, arranged next to the palace.

Ciechanowiec. Skansen museum of Podlasie-Mazovian wooden architecture.

In the Middle Ages, the borderland between Mazovia, Lithuania and Rus' was covered with dense forests, whose vestiges are the Augustów, Knyszyn and Białowieża forests. Białowieża Forest, which has retained its primeval character, is the best preserved complex of natural lowland woodlands in Central-Eastern Europe, occupying an area of 125 000 hectares. The western part of the Forest lies within Polish frontiers (58 000 hectares). More than a half of this terrain is taken up by oak and hornbearn,

with linden and maple. Significant areas are composed of mixed woods (pine, oak and spruce). Pine trees predominate on sandy soils, and marshland forests, basically black alder, prevail in undrained lowlands. Ash swamps stretch along the streams; alder mires, peatbogs and meadows abound. The local fauna is richly represented: 11 000 species have been recorded.

A part of Białowieża Forest between the Narewka and its tributary, the Hwoźna, belongs to the

Białowieża National Park (total area of 5 069 hectares, of which 4 747 hectares are under strict protection). The primeval woodland boasts of greatly differentiated vegetation. Numerous ancient trees are accompanied by fallen trunks overgrown with lichen, moss and fungi. Rare species include the lynx, elks, beavers, wolves, wild boar, badgers, roe deer, stags, otters and ermines; bird life is represented by the wood grouse, heath cocks, goshawks, black storks, cranes and sea eagles. The population of small rodents and insect-eating mammals is equally interesting. The Park is the natural habitat of the European bison, additionally bred in special reservations, as is the tarpan horse.

The changing owners of Białowieża Forest included the princes of Rus' and then of Lithuania, followed by the monarchs of Poland. After 1815, the Forest became the property of the tsars of Russia; it finally returned to the Polish state in 1921. For centuries, it was renowned for huge hunting expeditions. Before

tackling the Teutonic Knights in 1410, King Władysław Jagiełło and the Lithuanian Grand Duke Witold spent almost half a year hunting in Białowieża to make supplies of game. Barrels of salted and smoked meat fed an army of 100 000 men taking part in the victorious battle of Grunwald. An inscription on an obelisk in the Białowieża palace park informs that on 27 March 1752 42 bisons, 13 elks and numerous other wild animals were killed during a hunting expedition conducted by King August III.

During the 16th century, settlements began to penetrate into the Forest, and woodlands were cleared. Nonetheless, for centuries Białowieża continued to act as a source of revenue for the state treasury thanks to rich resources of timber, game and honey. Devastation and poaching during the partitions resulted in more serious damage, while the policy pursued during in the first world war by the German occupant incurred enormous losses. About 5 million cubic meters of valuable timber was

Białowieska Forest.

on the left:

Białowieża.
Hunting lodge.

Tykocin.
Church of the
Holy Trinity
from about 1454.

on the right:

Tykocin.
Synagogue interior
from about 1642.

felled, and great numbers of the wild animals were slaughtered, including almost all the bisons and all the elks. Research inaugurated in postwar Poland aimed to salvage the scourged fragments of the natural forest and to reintroduce the European bison. The second world war did not cause significant devastation, although the delineation of new state frontiers meant that a considerable part of the Forest now found itself in Belorussia. Immediately after the war, the task of rebuilding the ravaged country necessitated new clearings. Although the Forest area diminished over the centuries, a large part of the primeval woodland has survived to our times. The number of animal species has been seriously reduced by centuries-long hunts, poaching and wartime hostilities. Certain species, such as the anroch (*bos primigenius*), which became extinct already during the late 14th century, were lost forever. The last European bison fell prey to a poacher

in 1919. The postwar campaign to restore the species proved a success: in 1938, there were 30 bisons in Poland, fifteen of which survived the second world war. The outcome of the breeding policy was surprisingly satisfactory. The herd rapidly multiplied to such a degree that it has become too large to be supported by the Park. Some of the bisons have been moved to other reservations, others have been exported to zoological gardens abroad, and in certain cases permission is granted to shoot selected animals. The herd in Białowieża Forest now totals several hundred, the majority living at large. The elk has also been reinstated in the Forest, and the tarpan horse has been introduced into the reservation. (I. J. K.)

To the west of Białystok lies Tykocin, a Mazovian border castle-town, granted municipal status in 1425. In 1665, this former property of the Gasztold

family, King Zygmunt Augustus, and then Hetman Stefan Czarniecki, who added it to the dowry of his daughter, Aleksandra, became one of the residences of the Branickis. During the 18th century, the urban layout of the town was altered, and numerous buildings were erected or redesigned upon the initiative of Jan Klemens Branicki. This was the period of the origin of the most valuable extant monument – the Late Baroque missionary monastery with the church of the Holy Trinity, completed in 1742-1749. Older landmarks include a synagogue from 1642, remodelled in the 18th century, and one of the earliest war veteran homes in Poland, built in 1634-1638. Tykocin

languished during the 19th century; heavily destroyed during the second world war, it lost its municipal status in 1950, but remains the most attractive Baroque-Neoclassical town-planning and architectural complex in the voivodeship of Podlasie. (I. J. K.)

Białystok, the main industrial and cultural centre of north-eastern Poland, was probably founded by Gedymin, the Grand Duke of Lithuania, in the 14th century. Together with the Podlasie region, it was incorporated into the Polish Kingdom in 1569 and belonged to the starosta of Tykocin; in 1661, both the borough and the region were granted to

Siemiatycze.
Late Baroque
palace-type
monastic building.

on the left:

Białystok.
The Branicki Palace.

Święta Góra Grabarka.

on the right:

Ortel Królewski, wooden church of Our Lady of the Rosary.

Stefan Czarniecki. Finally, the borough passed into the possession of the Branickis to become a centre of their family estates. On the site of the old castle Tylman van Gameren designed a Baroque palace for the new owners (1691-1697). In 1728-1758, the palace was enlarged and remodelled into a Late Baroque aristocratic residence known as the "Versailles of Podlasie" (today: the seat of the Medical Academy). Jan Klemens Branicki stationed a garrison in Białystok and founded a military academy and schools for estate administra-

tors and boys. He also built a hospital and a theatre, and encouraged handicrafts and manufacturing. After Branicki's death, Białystok, which received municipal status in 1749, was acquired by the Potockis; in 1795, it became the property of the King of Prussia, and after the treatise of Tilsitz (1807) it was annexed into the Russian Empire. The growth of the 19th-century town was connected predominantly with the creation of the Białystok Textile Industrial Region. In inter-war Poland Białystok was the capital of a voivodeship.

During the second world war and the Nazi occupation, the town lost more than half of its population, almost the whole of its industry, and 80% of
all buildings. It owed postwar recovery to the
swift reconstruction and expansion of industry
and the town itself, as well as the establishment
of numerous administrative, academic and cultural
institutions. (I. J. K.)

Two Tartar villages have survived on the eastern
borderland of the voivodeship of Podlasie, an area

once belonging to Lithuania. Bohoniki dates back
to a 15th-century settlement, and Kruszyniany
was given to Kryczyński, captain of a Tartar
detachment, by King Jan III Sobieski whose life
was saved by the Tartar officer during the battle
of Parkany, waged on 7-9 October 1683 after the
siege of Vienna. The wooden, twin-towered
mosque in Kruszyniany comes from the 18th century. The village also possesses a Tartar cemetery
with tombstones inscribed in Arabic and the Latin
alphabet. (I. J. K.)

**Supraśl. Orthodox
monastery.**

on the left:
**Kruszyniany. Wooden
Tartar mosque.**

on pages 282-283:
**Biebrza National
Park.**

THE BALTIC LITTORAL AND LAKE DISTRICTS

A ugustów Forest (114 000 hectares, of which 6 300 hectares are in Lithuania and Belarus) stretches across the Augustów Plain, north of the Biebrza Basin. The forest stand is dominated by straight and tall pine trees, with considerable areas of dry wood-land; mixed forests with spruce are less frequent. Waterlogged areas are overgrown with alder. The Nazi policy of felling explains the young age of the trees. Apart from timber, Augustów Forest supplies considerable quantities of resin as well as plentiful mushrooms, blueberries, wild strawberries and cran-berries. Prior to the partitions of Poland the Forest constituted royal property providing extensive hunt-ing grounds. Similarly as in the case of Białowieża Forest, supplies of game were prepared on the eve of the battle of Grunwald, and hunting expeditions were held by King Zygmunt Augustus and Stefan Batory. During the January Uprising (1863-1864), the Forest served as a base for numerous insurgent detachments; it played the same role for World War II partisans. Augustów Forest is crossed by the Czarna Hańcza, a tributary of the Niemen, whose mouth lies beyond the borders of Poland. The sources of the Hańcza flow southwards from the moraine elevations of the Suwałki Lake District into Lake Hańcza, from which they emerge as a uniform river. The water of this picturesque, meandering river is so pure that salmon is bred along almost its whole length. The Augustów Canal connects the Czarna Hańcza with the Biebrza-Narew river system to create a single water route across north-eastern Poland. The river constitutes one of the most attrac-tive canoe routes in the country, with numerous boathouses, harbours and camping sites. Passing

on the right:

Lake Śniardwy.

through the lakes and the Augustów Canal the route leads to the town of Augustów, the main recreational centre of the region. Surrounded by woodlands, it is situated on the south-western edge of Augustów Forest, over the River Netta, and between lakes Necko, Białe and Sajno. Augustów developed around an inn founded in 1526 by Jan Radziwiłł on the main land route linking Grodno and Prussia. In 1546, Queen Bona, the wife of Zygmunt the Old, suggested establishing a borough to be named Zygmuntów after the royal heir, Zygmunt Augustus. The new town, however, came to be known as Augustów, thus commemorating the second name of the Prince who soon afterwards (1548) mounted his father's throne. (I. J. K.)

When in post-partition Poland the Vistula estuary was annexed by Prussia and high customs duties were introduced along the frontier with the Kingdom of Poland, the traditional river route proved no longer convenient for foreign trade. The authorities of the autonomous Kingdom decided to become independent of Prussian ports and to reach the Baltic by means of a new waterway; this necessitated the construction of a canal linking the Vistula basin with the Niemen *via* the Narew, the Biebrza and the Netta. The initiator of the Augustów Canal was Prince Ksawery Drucki-Lubecki, the Minister of the Treasury; the author of the project was Ignacy Prądzyński, under whose supervision work on the canal was started in 1825. Interrupted by the November Uprising, construction was renewed by the Bank of Poland and completed in 1839. The length of the canal between the Biebrza and the Niemen totals 101 km, 19 of which are now outside the Polish frontier. The canal system is composed of the canalised Netta, the Augustów lakes, and a regulated part of the Czarna Hańcza. Eighteen stone locks raise the water level from the Biebrza to Augustów by 15 m, and lower it from Augustów to the Niemen by 41 m. Traffic on the canal was lively for the first twenty years; afterwards, the waterway lost its economic significance, mainly due to the competing railways and the omission to complete other links. The fact that the Biebrza and the upper

Narew remain unregulated means that the canal possesses no connections with other water routes in Poland. It is used for tourist purposes, and timber is still floated from Augustów Forest to a sawmill located on Lake Białe. Boat trips are arranged for the numerous holidaymakers visiting the Augustów lakes. In 1968, the canal was placed under protection as a monument of hydro - engineering.

The Forest is rich in fauna. Rare species include the lynx, beavers and elks, as well as the blue hare. Beaver dams surround Lake Wigry; the presence of these animals is evidenced by the chopped down

Augustów Canal.
Lock in Przewięź.

on the left:

Giżycko, port.

**Lake Wigry.
Cameldolite
monastery,
hermitages.**

Lake Wigry, situated at the northern edge of Augustów Forest, is considered to be Poland's most beautiful. With an area of 2 187 hectares it is up to 73 m deep and 3,5 km wide. The irregular shape of the lake resembles the letter "S", and its length along this axis totals almost 18 km. The Wigry coastline is well-developed, with numerous bays and peninsulas, of which the largest – Wysoki Węgiel – stretches for about 4 km. The largely forested and hilly banks are easily accessible. The clean waters are rich in fish, including the rare lavaret. The surrounding country-side is full of many smaller lakes, which were origi-nally the bays of Lake Wigry. The largest – Białe Wigierskie – has an area of 100 hectares. Wigry is composed of three parts known as *plosy*, the western-most of which, in the vicinity of the village of Bryzgiel, is the most varied, with a high bank offer-ing magnificent views of inlets, peninsulas and islands. The lower, northern shore borders with thick forests concealing several highly diversified small lakes: Okrągłe, Długie and Muliste, which comprise a strict reservation. The central *ploso* of Lake Wigry has low, forested shores with deep inlets, while the third, northern section of the lake is dotted with vil-lages. Hańcza Bay, where the Czarna Hańcza flows into the lake, includes the Stary Folwark beaver sanctuary, an animal reservation with beaver dams as well as water and nearshore plants. A second beaver reservation at Zakęty lies at the south-east-ern end of the lake in Krzyżacka Bay. Since 1989, Lake Wigry and its surroundings have been func-tioning as the Wigry National Park. The beauty of the lake and its still unspoiled natural surroundings attract amateurs of water sports and summer holi-daymakers, who enjoy the facilities offered in the numerous resorts.

The former Cameldolite church of the Immaculate Conception of the Holy Virgin Mary on the northern side of Lake Wigry soars high above the waters and can be seen from afar. The Cameldolites were settled on Królewska (Royal) Island by King Władysław IV Vasa. In 1704-1745, they built a monastery complex and linked the island with the mainland by creating a dyke. The resulting peninsula became known as

tree trunks lying on the shores of the lake and used for building dams. Decimated already before the Great War, the elk herds returned to the Forest after 1960 from the nearby Czerwone (Red) Marsh. Wild boar, deer and foxes abound, although the wolf, which was still well represented in the area at the end of World War II, has all but disappeared. Bird life is in abundance; this is the nesting area of the rare wood grouse and the mating site of the heath cock and the woodcock. The presence of the extremely rare black stork is particularly notewo-rthy. A great variety of smaller mammals, amphi-bians, reptiles and insects is accompanied by fish teeming in the pure waters. Certain local species are protected. (I. J. K.)

the Klasztorny (Monastery) Peninsula. Up to the cassation of the order in 1800, the Cameldolites farmed their estates, attracted settlers, and set up sawmills, mills, breweries and distilleries; they also smelted iron from the local morass ore. The Baroque church, destroyed during the two world wars, was restored together with the devastated monastery buildings (the so-called Royal Manor and hermitages), which today serve as a summer retreat. (I. J. K.)

Originally, the territory between the Great Mazurian Lakes and the Niemen-Biebrza valley was inhabited by the Sudovians, a Baltic people who made frequent sorties into neighbouring lands. During the 13th century, the Sudovians were weakened by the retaliatory attacks of the Poles and the Ruthenians; the ultimate blow was dealt by the Teutonic Order in 1283. Vestiges of strongholds, burial mounds and local place names are all that remain of the Sudovians. The land became overgrown with thick forests and was captured by the Lithuanians after years-long battles waged against the Teutonic Order. The dukes of Lithuania and, subsequently, the Polish kings who hunted here, granted parts of the forests to their feudal lords. The meadows, wild beehives and richly stocked lakes attracted Lithuanian and later Polish settlers. In the second half of the 17th century, Dominican and Cameldolite monasteries took over the colonisation of the forests. In 1602, Jerzy Grodziński donated to the Dominicans the former estates of the Wiśniowiecki and Sapieha families, which he had purchased in 1593, together with the town of Juriewo, whose name was changed to Sejny. The monks opened a printing shop, and in 1610-1619 erected a monastery and a church, which in 1760 was remodelled in the Late Baroque style. From 1807, the town of Sejny, rebuilt after the 17th-century Swedish invasion, was the seat of a county, and in 1818-1925 – of a bishopric. Today, the population of this tourist centre includes a sizable Lithuanian community. (I. J. K.)

At the end of the 17th century, the Wigry Cameldolites founded the village of Suwałki next to a ford

across the Czarna Hańcza river at the north-western edge of the Augustów Plain. The settlement was granted urban rights in 1715. The third partition of Poland (1795) granted Suwałki to Prussia, and the monastic estates were confiscated. In 1807, Suwałki was incorporated into the Grand Duchy of Warsaw, and in 1815 – into the Kingdom of Poland, where it became the seat of the authorities of the voivodeship (from 1837 – the gubernia) of Augustów. In 1866, the town became the seat of the gubernia of Suwałki. It grew significantly during the 19th century, when the major part of its historical monuments was built. The famous poetess Maria Konopnicka was born here in 1842. During the second world war, the town was annexed by Eastern Prussia and acted as a

Sejny. Church of the Visitation of the Holy Virgin Mary.

Piska Forest. Resistance centre. Postwar development entailed the construction of new housing estates and industrial enterprises.

The most easterly part of northern Poland comprises the Suwałki Lake District, an area of steep moraine ridges strewn with boulders deposited by glaciers which descended from Scandinavia. Cattle is grazed in the meadows and pastures, and land cultivation is of secondary importance. Deep depressions harbour picturesque lakes. The highest and most beautiful part of this region is the Suwałki Landscape Park with Lake Hańcza, the deepest lake in Poland (108m), the Smolnickie lakes, particularly Lake Jaczno, and the charming Lake Kleszczewskie. (I. J. K.)

The central part of the Mazurian Lake District and, simultaneously, its main tourist area is the Land of the Great Mazurian Lakes, a wide depression stretching to the south. The lakes, situated along its axis and linked by 19th-century canals, form a water system occupying an area of 486 sq. km, of which 302 sq. km belong to interconnected lakes. The most northerly Lake Mamry, Poland's second largest (nearly 105 sq. km), is composed of several parts bearing different names. The western part, known as Lake Dobskie, is famous for a cormorant island – a reservation and nesting site. To the east, Lake Dobskie is linked with Lake Dargin. The Great Lakes series ends with the southernmost Lake Nidzkie; in the shape of

a deformed letter "C", it is enfolded by Pisz Forest. The lake shore accommodates a number of holiday centres, the largest of which is Ruciane, located at its northern end. Lake Nidzkie is joined by a chain of smaller lakes with Lake Beldany, into which the River Krutynia which flows from the Mrągowo Lake District through a number of lakes, creating an extremely popular canoe route, some 90 km long, discharges itself. Lake Śniardwy, Poland's largest, with an area of 11 383 hectares, is a shallow lake (averaging 5,9 m) with four islands and a well-developed shoreline with numerous bays. The rather low shores are in places outright flat and waterlogged. To the north-west, Lake Śniardwy is connected with

the small Lake Łuknajno, a water and wading fowl sanctuary with a wild swan nesting reservation; to the west, Lake Śniardwy joins Lake Mikołajskie. It fills the central section of a narrow gully, whose southern part is composed of Lake Bałdany, while the northern part comprises Lake Tałty. At the narrow neck between lakes Mikołajki and Tałty there lies Mikołajki, a former Mazurian village expanded in the late 19th century as a holiday resort in the very heart of the Great Mazurian Lakes. Numerous tourist and recreation centres have been built on the shores of Lake Niegocin, linked by canals with Late Tałty in the north and Lake Mamry in the south. The whole system of interconnected lakes offers routes for

Mikołajki, shores of Lake Mikołajskie.

on pages 292-293:

Mazurian landscape in the region of Wilkasy.

on the right:

Święta Lipka.
Jesuit church.

Święta Lipka.
Interior of the
Jesuit church,
organs.

Święta Lipka,
arcades.

inland sailing sports and water tourism; it is also well known for lake fishing. (I. J. K.)

The Jesuit church and monastery at Święta Lipka were constructed among the lakes and forests of Mazuria in 1687-1692. The designer, Jerzy Ertli of Wilno, built a three-nave basilica with an imposing twin-towered façade. The interiors have retained their uniform Late Baroque character. Special attention is due to the magnificent organ from 1721 and the polychrome by Maciej Jan Mejer of Lidzbark. The painter revealed great adroitness in evoking illusion: the nave wall has been "prolonged" by a painted architectural motif, and the vaulting appears to change into a cupola supported on painted columns. The artist's grasp of geometry made it possible for the observer to become uncertain where architecture ends and illusion begins. Mejer based himself on Italian models of illusionistic painting, and built his compositions exclusively by resorting to colour which he applied spontaneously, with the élan of a true colourist. The church, well-known for its patron-saint festivities, is surrounded by galleries

with chapels at the corners and numerous figures of saints placed above the wall. (P. T.)

For centuries, the bishop's castle in Lidzbark Warmiński was not only a seat of Polish bishops, but also a significant Polish cultural centre influencing the furthest reaches of Warmia. Its last resident, the acclaimed Enlightenment-era poet and novelist Ignacy Krasicki, was evicted from the castle by the Prussians in 1795. The building stands at the confluence of the Łyna and Symsarna rivers, and was constructed throughout the whole second half of the 14th century. The regular brick rectangle has an inner courtyard encircled with single-storey galleries. A tower and three turrets at the corners of the castle originate from the late 15th century. Ornamental stellar vaults and frescoes from the 14th-16th century decorate the stately chambers on the first storey. The castle chapel reveals an unexpected Rococo outfitting from the 1770s. (P. T.)

The historic land of Warmia in the basin of the Łyna and the Pasłęka took its name from an Old Pruthen-

ian tribe of the Warmowie. In the 13th century, it was conquered by the Teutonic Knights, who established a bishopric. During the 15th century, the local gentry and townspeople joined the Prussian Alliance, established in 1440 to oppose the Order. An uprising against the Knights broke out in 1454, and the Alliance gained control of numerous towns supporting a merger with Poland. The Polish monarch, Ka-zimierz Jagiellon, announced the incorporation of Prussia into the Crown and declared war on the Teutonic Knights, which thirteen years later ended with a division of the Teutonic state. By virtue of the peace of Toruń (1466) Warmia became part of Royal Prussia. After the first partition of Poland, it belonged to Prussia and then to Germany; in 1945, it was restored to Poland. (I. J. K.)

Lidzbark Warmiński. Castle of the bishops of Warmia.

on the left:

Orneta. Interior of the church of St. John the Evangelist.

Orneta, located to the west of Lidzbark, was the property of the bishops of Warmia and one of their economic centres, granted municipal status in 1313. In 1440, it joined the Prussian Alliance. Under Polish rule, the town enjoyed considerable prosperity, only to decline after incorporation into Prussia. The most outstanding historic building is the Gothic church of St. John the Baptist, erected before 1379 and with an interior from the 15th-18th century.

The origins of Olsztyn, picturesquely situated amid hills and lakes, go back to 1334, when the Warmia chapter built a castle on the Łyna, in a sparsely populated woodland region. A settlement arose around the castle and in 1353 was granted municipal rights.

Olsztyn became a member of the Prussian Alliance and subsequently flourished as a Polish town. In 1516-1521, the administrator of Olsztyn on behalf of the Warmia chapter was Nicholas Copernicus, who in 1520 commanded the town's defence against the Teutonic Knights after the Order declared war on Poland so as to free itself from feudal dependence. Incorporation into Prussia negatively affected the economic life of Olsztyn, which recovered during the 19th century thanks to a railway junction and the rank of a regency capital (1911). Despite the official Germanisation policy, intensified at the end of the 19th century, Olsztyn remained an important centre of the Polish national and cultural movement, and in 1921 it became the seat of the Union of Poles in Ger-

■ **Olsztyn. Cathedral of St. James.**

■ **Pasym. Protestant church with the celebrated organs.**

on the left:

Olsztyn. New town hall in the Dutch Renaissance style, beginning of the 20th century.

**Olsztynek.
Museum of Folk
Architecture.**

after the peace of Toruń (1466) it remained part of vassal Teutonic Prussia (after 1526 known as Ducal Prussia). Contacts with Poland were maintained: Polish settlers kept coming, 17th-century local pastors were Poles, and trade with Poland was lively. In 1656, the borough was destroyed by the Tartars; the wars, fires and pestilence of the 18th century contributed to decline. The construction of a sugar refinery at the close of the 19th century revived Pasym somewhat, but the second world war left it ruined and depopulated. In 1950, the town lost its urban status. Numerous monuments ranging from the 14th to the 19th century have been preserved, and a stronghold exemplifying Western Baltic culture (6th-11th century) stands nearby.

Olsztynek, founded by the Teutonic Knights in 1359 next to a fortified castle in the south-western part of the Olsztyn Lake District, was situated in the vicinity of Olsztyn, within the former territory of the Old Pruthenian tribe of the Sasinowie. Settlers from Mazovia arrived in large numbers throughout the 14th century, and Poles remained predominant in the town; consequently, during the Polish-Teutonic wars of the 15th and 16th century the burghers and the local gentry aimed, unsuccessfully, at achieving a union with the Crown. At the time of the Reformation, Olsztynek became an important centre of Polish Protestantism in Mazuria. Krzysztof Celestyn Mrongowiusz (Mrongovius), the eminent lexicographer and defender of the Polish language, was born in Olsztynek in 1764. German impact did not prevail until the end of the 19th century. The town was seriously damaged during both world wars, although several old buildings remained intact. The open-air Museum of Folk Architecture, displaying examples of rare regional architecture from Warmia and Mazuria, is a notable tourist attraction. (I. J. K.)

many. The 1939-1945 period witnessed mass-scale arrests and executions of Polish activists. Olsztyn suffered serious damage in 1945, when 40% of the town was destroyed. Rebuilt and enlarged upon its return to Poland, it is the leading economic and cultural focal point of Warmia and Mazuria. (I. J. K.)

Pasym, 30 km south-east of Olsztyn in the Olsztyn Lake District, was founded by the Teutonic Knights. Granted municipal rights in 1386, the town joined the Prussian Alliance and surrendered to Poland, but

The battle waged in 1410 near the village of Grunwald, to the south of Ostróda, proved to be a turning point in centuries-long hostilities involving the Polish Kingdom and the Teutonic Order. The two great armies taking part in one of mediaeval Europe's

largest land battle were the Polish-Lithuanian forces led by King Władysław Jagiełło, and the Knights of the Teutonic Order under the Grand Master, Ulrich von Jungingen. The victory won by Jagiełło resulted in the decimation of the Knights and the death of the Grand Master. The military success, albeit insufficiently exploited, put an end to Teutonic expansion, reinforced the political union between Poland and the Grand Duchy of Lithuania, enhanced the international prestige of the Polish monarchy, and is kept alive in the memories of Poles. The 550th anniversary of the victory was commemorated by a monument unveiled on the battlefield. (I. J. K.)

During the Middle Ages, the Chełmno Lake District, a region bordering with the Vistula, Osa and Drwęca river valleys, was the object of rivalry between Mazovia and Pruthenian tribes. The Land of Chełmno, granted in 1228 by Konrad, the Duke of Mazovia, to the Teutonic Order, became a base for sorties into Pruthenia, which the Knights conquered, and into Poland. The system of fortified castles built by the Order augmented control over the province. Radzyń Chełmiński is a small town in the Chełmno Lake District. Visitors are advised to see the Gothic parish church from the first half of the 14th century and the ruins of a Teutonic Order castle from the

Radzyń Chełmiński. Ruins of a 14th-century Teutonic Order castle.

on pages 302-303:

Golub-Dobrzyń. Castle.

13th-14th century. In 1224, the castle-town became the property of Christian, the Bishop of Prussia. In 1231, its new owners, the Teutonic Order, constructed an imposing castle – the seat of a military district. Conquered by the Poles in 1410, Radzyń for a short time belonged to the Prussian Alliance and in 1466 returned to Poland. By then, the Teutonic castle had been destroyed as a result of wars with the Order. In 1772, Chełmno was seized by the Prussians, and finally restored to Poland in 1920. Another seat of the Teutonic Order military commander was the castle in Golub – Dobrzyń on the Drwęca, later the residence of Anna Vasa, who remodelled the castle in the Renaissance style. The partition-era frontier between Russia and Prussia isolated Golub from its former suburb of Dobrzyń, which developed into a separate town. In 1951, Golub and Dobrzyń merged once again into single urban centre. The assorted

ceremonies and historical spectacles, including knights' tournaments, held in the majestic castle, today a tourist hostel and a regional museum, draw numerous tourists. (I. J. K.)

Chełmno is the capital of a region bearing the same name in the voivodeship of Kujawy-Pomerania. As early as the 10th century it was the site of a castle-town and then the seat of the local castellan. A missionary bishopric, established to introduce Christianity to Pruthenia, was established in Chełmno in 1215. Soon afterwards, the whole region became the property of the Teutonic Knights, with Chełmno originally playing the role of the main centre. In 1233, the town was granted municipal rights, which subsequently served as a model for the *locatio* of other West Pomeranian and Mazovian boroughs. During the 14th century, Chełmno developed into a large

■ **Toruń. Church of St. James.**

■ **Chełmno. Late Renaissance town hall from 1567-1570.**

on the left:

Chełmno. Parish church of the Assumption of the Holy Virgin Mary.

Toruń. Panorama.

trading centre and joined the Hanseatic League; in 1466, it returned to Poland. The Chełmno Academy functioned in the 1386-1697 period. As part of the Prussian partition area (1772-1920) Chełmno remained one of the active focal points of the Polish national movement in Pomerania. The preserved mediaeval urban layout is composed of town walls (17 towers and the Grudziądzka Gate) encircling a complex of historical buildings, including the Gothic parish church (1290-1333) and the 16th-century Mannerist town hall raised on a Gothic base and graced with ornamental attics, redesigned in the 19th century. (I. J. K.)

Toruń is a unique example of mediaeval architecture: a well-preserved urban layout from the second half of the 13th century with more than 350 Gothic buildings. Although it lies 200 km from the Baltic coast, the town prospered predominantly thanks to foreign trade made possible by its convenient location on the navigable Vistula. In the 14th century, Toruń joined the Hanseatic League, and its inhabitants played a leading role in resistance against the Teutonic Order which imposed high taxes and restricted trade with Poland. In 1466, Toruń returned to the Crown, and during the 16th century became a major centre of the Reformation in Poland.

The impressive post-Franciscan church of the Holy Virgin Mary (1350-1370) commands the Old Town skyline. Initially, each of the three naves was covered with a separate roof; the present roof was not built until the end of the 18th century. The hall church, with an interior 27 m high, is an original construction rarely encountered in Gothic architecture. The naves were usually enclosed by powerful buttresses, but in this case the exterior walls are smooth since buttresses were introduced into the interior, decorated with 14th-century polychrome. The stellar and floral motifs of the vaulting symbolise heavenly paradise, while the walls display scenes from the New Testament and the pillars are embellished with figures of the saints. The style of the murals suggests artists connected with Bohemia. The Early Baroque tombstone of Anna Vasa, sister of King Zygmunt III Vasa, was built in 1636.

A large part of the Market Square is taken up by the town hall which originates from the late 14th century when several buildings, including the cloth hall, stalls, town scales and law chambers were combined into one. At the beginning of the 17th century, the Gdańsk architect Antoni van Opbergen added gables and corner turrets. The town hall, with its fine proportions and walls divided by means of high niches,

Toruń.
So-called palace of the bishops of Kujawy – a Baroque residence from the end of the 17th century.

**Grudziądz.
Panorama.**

is reminiscent of its Late Gothic counterparts from the Low Countries. The interiors, redesigned in the 18th century, have retained much of their earlier character and provide an excellent background for the rich collections of the Toruń museum: mediaeval art, crafts, arms and armour, and Polish art from the 19th and 20th century. (P. T.)

Long stretches of mediaeval town walls with gates and towers face the Vistula. The three Gothic churches include the distinctive church of St. James in the New Town. Built in 1309-1321, its slender sil-

houette is best viewed from the side of the presbytery, which is closed by means of a simple wall. The architecture was enhanced by glazed ceramic details with polychrome. The interiors contain valuable outfitting from the 14th to the 18th century, including Gothic frescoes, paintings and sculptures. One of the Gothic town houses to survive in Toruń is the house in which Nicholas Copernicus was born in 1477: a typical example of a Hanseatic town residence, with a façade enhanced with gables, niches and colourful painted ornaments. Another house in the Old Town Market Square displays a Baroque façade from 1697,

featuring lavish floral motifs. The "House under the Star" (today: the Museum of Oriental Art) has preserved a beautiful spiral, wooden staircase. (P. T.)

A panoramic view of Grudziądz, seen from the Vistula, reveals a picturesque complex of granaries, predominantly mediaeval, which at one time formed part of the municipal defence walls. From the late 13th century until 1466, Grudziądz belonged to the Teutonic Order; afterwards, it became a royal town and the site of the dietines convened by the gentry of Royal Prussia. (P. T.)

Kwidzyń Castle, built in the first half of the 14th century and the seat of a bishopric created in 1284, was connected with the local cathedral. The castle was designed on the ground plan of a regular square with four corner towers and an inner courtyard with galleries. A long porch leads to a latrine tower known as a dansker. The cathedral was fortified, and contains a spacious double-nave crypt beneath the presbytery. A mosaic from 1380 has survived above the porch, and Gothic polychrome has been preserved inside. (P. T.)

Kwidzyn.
Castle courtyard.

on pages 310-311:

Malbork.
Teutonic Order
castle.

The Teutonic Order erected its seat in Malbork in several stages. The earliest buildings on the River Nogat were constructed at the end of the 13th century. In 1309, the Grand Master moved his residence from Venice to Malbork, which he decided to turn into a state capital. The fortifications were intensively enlarged during the 14th century, and a Great Refectory was constructed in the middle castle together with the Grand Master's residence and the church of St. Bartholomew. At the end of that century, a four-storey residential tower was raised, together with the Summer and Winter Refectories, whose high vaults are supported by granite pillars. The chapel of the Holy Virgin Mary, an exceptionally valuable example of Gothic art, was added in the high castle together with the Great Chapter House.

The castle was encircled by four lines of fortifications. After Poland seized Malbork in 1457, the castle served as the seat for the local starosta. Greatest damage was incurred under Prussian rule, when the castle was adapted into depots and barracks by demolishing part of the complex. A gradual reconstruction was not initiated until after 1817, and was continued after 1945, a year which caused extensive devastation. Today, this largest Gothic fortress in Europe is a museum of brilliant architectural solutions. The Amber Museum deserves the visitor's special attention. (P. T.)

The Pomeranian castle-town of Gniew on the Vistula is situated between Kwidzyń and Malbork. In 1229, the region of Gniew was granted to the Cistercians of

Oliwa, and in 1276 – to the Teutonic Knights, who erected a castle, the seat of their military commander, conceived as the first bridgehead of the Order on the west bank of the Vistula. During the Thirteen Years War (1454-1466) Gniew became the main centre of the Knights' resistance. After its return to Poland in 1466, the town prospered thanks to trade on the Vistula, and became the seat of the local starosta. In 1667-1699, Gniew belonged to the Sobieski family; Jan Sobieski rebuilt the borough, extensively destroyed by the Swedes. Gniew lost its original significance during the partition era, and today is a small industrial centre. The town has preserved the mediaeval layout, parts of the defensive walls (14th century), a 14th-century Gothic parish church, Late Gothic arcaded houses in the Market Square (14th and 15th century) and a Gothic castle, remodelled during the reign of Jan Sobieski (today: a Department of the Archaeological Museum in Gdańsk). Historical spectacles and knights' tournaments are held in the castle since 1993. (I. J. K.)

The Elbląg Elevation, a series of low hills with beautiful forests of beech and oak, adjoins the southern part of the Vistula Estuary. The central fragment of the Elevation is farmed. The large industrial town of Elbląg lies on a river of that name, along a borderline between the Elevation and the Żuławy depression. This former important member of the Hanseatic League lost its status in the 17th century, when the port silted up and wars ravaged the town; it revived in the mid-19th century, when industrialisation followed the opening of railway links and the Elbląg Canal. Built in 1845-1860, the canal connects Elbląg with Ostróda and a series of lakes in the Iława Lake District. The northern prolongation of the canal is composed of the shallow Lake Drużno (part of a former bay) and the River Elbląg, which flows into the Vistula Estuary. The canal possesses two locks and five slipways – unique in Europe. Ships, boats or rafts are placed on special platforms which, by moving on the land on rails, transfer them to different levels of the water route (from 13 m to 24,5 m). Today, the canal is used almost exclusively by tourists. (I. J. K.)

on the left:

**Frombork.
Gothic cathedral of
the Assumption of
the Holy Virgin Mary
and St. Andrew.**

Żuławy.
Rape field.

The town of Frombork, built at the eastern end of the Elbląg Elevation over the Vistula Estuary, belonged to the bishops of Warmia; since 1278, it was the seat of a bishopric and the centre of a chapter. Nicholas Copernicus resided and worked in Formbork in 1512-1516 and 1522-1543; here he wrote his monumental *De revolutionibus orbium coelestium*, and here he was buried. The most valuable among the preserved historical monuments is the cathedral complex, including the Gothic cathedral built in 1329-1388 and a tower from the second half of the 14th century, containing the rooms where Copernicus lived. In 1973, the 500th anniversary of the astronomer's birth was commemorated by a monument unveiled at the foot of cathedral hill. (I. J. K.)

The Vistula Estuary is separated from the open sea by the Vistula Reef, a sand bar some 50 km long and

created over the centuries by wind and surf. To the west, the Reef separates the Bay of Gdańsk from the Vistula delta, known as Żuławy. In the past, the bay was much more extensive, but gradually buried under the Vistula outwash it grew shallow and withdrew to the north. Consequently, the area of the estuary, which in the 13th century stretched all the way to Lake Drużno, at the time a bay of the estuary, has shrunk considerably. A large lake lay to the south-east of Gdańsk. The reef was broken in several places, thus creating a direct connection between the estuary and the sea. As the bay receded, the Żuławy delta widened and its depressions gave way to waterlogged marshes; the higher terrains became overgrown with dense river-meadow woods. Already in the 12th and 13th century, the fertile soil, produced by the river outwash in the course of centuries under the cover of the woods, drew settlers to

Gdańsk. Town hall.

on the right:

**Gdańsk.
Mariacka Street.**

higher ground. During the 14th century, the Teutonic Knights embarked upon draining the Żuławy area, a task which they entrusted to specially invited settlers from northern Germany, Friesland and The Netherlands, experienced in land drainage. The river banks were regulated, embankments, canals and ditches were formed, and windmills, which were used to work the pumps, were constructed. The fens were divided into polders suitable for cultivation. By the 16th century, the Vistula Żuławy fenland sup-

plied Gdańsk, Elbląg and Malbork with food.

In the 19th century, the old mud buckets and pumps driven by windmills were replaced by steam pumps, which, in turn, gave way to 20th-century electric appliances. Centuries of assorted undertakings drained the entire delta, i. e., 174 000 hectares, of which 47 hectares comprised a depression up to 1.8 m below sea level. At the end of the second world war, the retreating German armies blew up the embankments and drainage installations, thus flooding

40 000 hectares of farmland and causing a further 32 000 to become waterlogged. A major part of the resultant bogs became overgrown with 3 metre-high reeds, and weeds spread across the remaining land. At the time, the Żuławy fens resembled more the wilderness they had been more than six centuries ago than the recently thriving farmland. Despite myriad obstacles, by 1949 the fens were drained and recultivated, drainage installations were modernised, and state farms were set up. Today, wheat, sugar beet and rape-seed are grown, and cattle is grazed in the Żuławy pastures and meadows. Numerous examples of historic architecture include skeleton-construction churches and houses, many of which feature arcades, as well as Dutch-type mills. (I. J. K.)

The archaeologically documented settlement and cultural history of Gdańsk, Poland's largest port, goes back to the Stone Age. The historical beginnings of the borough are associated with Mieszko I, who conquered the mouth of the Vistula; the first written record originates from the year 997. During the period of the feudal fragmentation of the Polish state into provinces Gdańsk was the capital of a sovereign duchy. In 1225, it was granted a *locatio* privilege according to the law of Lübeck, and the 14th century witnessed the emergence of four independent urban communes: the settlement of Osiek, nearest to the castle, which was granted urban rights in 1312, the Main Town, whose urban rights were based on the law of Chełmno (1343), the New Town, founded by the Teutonic Knights in 1380, and the Old Town, rebuilt in 1308. From the 13th century, Gdańsk was a member of the Hanseatic League and conducted extensive trade with West Europe (Flanders, the Netherlands, England, France) and Scandinavia. The port was considerably enlarged, and in 1364 the Great Mill (Wielki Młyn) was built on the river Radunia. Gdańsk exported woodland products (fur, potash, tar), metal, fish and rye, and imported cloth, salt, salted herrings, wine and fruit from southern Europe. The crafts flourished.

Increasingly prosperous and powerful, Gdańsk could no longer tolerate the rule of the Teutonic Order,

especially the heavy taxation, intervention in urban issues, and trade competition. In 1440, the town joined the Prussian Alliance, and in 1454 it toppled the governance of the Order and fought on the Polish side in the Thirteen Years War (1454-1466); its support was rewarded by numerous privileges. The division into several rivalling communes was abolished, and Gdańsk became a prominent economic centre of the Commonwealth, concentrating more than 80% of all foreign trade. It also fulfilled important production functions, making cloth, furniture, metal goods and arms, which were stored in the Great Armoury, built in 1603-1605. Science and art progressed. The numerous scholars working in Gdańsk included the renowned astronomer Jan Heweliusz (Johannes

Gdańsk.
Great Armoury.

on the left:
Gdańsk.
Crane on the river
Motława.

Gdańsk. Town hall, Red Hall.

Hevelius, 1611-1687). Acclaimed architects, sculptors and painters enhanced the town with their magnificent Renaissance and Baroque works. The Swedish wars and the economic decline of the country in the 17th-18th century undermined further development. Incorporated into Prussia, the post-1793 Gdańsk was cut off from the Polish markets and lost its former significance. Revival came in the second half of the 19th century when railway lines were laid, the port was expanded and the shipbuilding industry grew. Between the wars, Gdańsk enjoyed the status of a Free City. Heavily damaged (55%) during World War II, it returned to Poland in

1945 and was rapidly rebuilt. Special attention was paid to the restoration of historical monuments, the most magnificent being those in the Main Town, once again dominated by the massive Late Gothic church of the Holy Virgin Mary, raised in stages between 1347 and 1502. (I. J. K.)

In 1612-1614, Abraham van den Blocke designed the Golden Gate, which leads to Długa Street, the main thoroughfare of the city. The bright stone elevation with the classical arrangement of columns and entablature suggests Italian influence, but this would be a superficial supposition since the stone lintels dividing the façade decorated with circular and cone-shaped motifs reflect the Mannerist spirit. The reconstructed sculptures adorning the balustrade are personifications of Peace, Freedom, Wealth and Fame. The adjacent residence of the St. George brotherhood, an association of Gdańsk patricians, was erected in 1487-1494 by Georg Glotau in place of a demolished section of the defence walls. This exceptionally beautiful Late Gothic building features an exquisitely composed façade and a stately hall on the upper floor. The Gothic Court of Arthur was built at the end of 15th century; its façade was first redesigned in the Italian Renaissance style in connection with a visit of King Zygmunt August, and assumed its present-day appearance when in 1616-1618 Abraham van den Blocke combined Gothic forms with Low Countries Mannerism. The splendid portal with the likenesses of Zygmunt III and Władysław IV as well as statues of classical heroes famed for integrity and devotion to the homeland, personifications of Justice and Might in the attic niches, and a statue of Fortune crowning the gable, reflect the ideological programme of this seat of the Gdańsk patricians: the favours of rulers and the virtues of citizens will secure eternal good fortune for the borough. Those guidelines are supplemented by the fountain standing in front of the Court of Arthur with a figure of Neptune, also designed by van den Blocke the Younger in 1604, but not unveiled until 1633. (P. T.)

The town hall of the Main Town, standing in Długi Targ (Long Market), was the most important public building in Gdańsk. Its oldest part originates from 1379-1382, but the present-day shape and lofty tower, which clearly refer to the late mediaeval town halls of the Netherlands, were granted a century later. When the Gothic cupola of the tower burned down, Dirk Daniels built the present-day one, which in 1561 was crowned with the gilt figure of King Zygmunt August and a carillon. At the end of the 16th century, Anton van Opberghen, the designer of the Armoury, remodelled the façade in a thoroughly Mannerist mode and totally refurbished the interiors.

Unfortunately, fires and a partial demolition of the town hall in 1945 ruined the interiors, and years later, despite the efforts of conservators, only the Grand Hall, also known as the Red Hall, regained its original appearance. This most outstanding Mannerist interior in Poland was designed almost entirely by artists from the Low Countries (1591-1611). Willem van der Meer of Ghent built the superb fireplace, Hans Vredeman de Vries painted a series of allegorical scenes adorning the walls, and Isaac van den Blocke, son of the sculptor Willem, conceived the unique ceiling decoration composed of 25 paintings dominated by the centrally placed *Apotheosis of the*

Gdańsk.

Court of Arthur.

Union of Gdańsk with Poland. Displayed in heavy, carved gilt frames, the compositions echo the Mannerist interior of the Doge's Palace in Venice, which at the time remained an unparalleled model for all European port cities. The paintings were mounted by Simon Hoerle, a carver from Gdańsk and the author of the inlaid doors and benches standing next to the walls. The Red Hall presents a well-conceived, albeit complex programme evoking ethical and political motifs pertaining to civic virtues and the situation and vital interests of Gdańsk. (P. T.)

Late Gothic brick gables distinguish the post-Franciscan church of the Holy Trinity, built at the beginning of the 16th century. The Gothic chambers of the former monastery house the collections of the National Museum. (P.T.)

Growing international trade increased traffic in the port of Gdańsk, which by the mid-17th century was handling over 2 000 ships annually. Already in the 14th century, the old port on the Motława was widened, and in the 17th century a new port was constructed at the mouth of the river Leniwka. The number of assorted port facilities and buildings also increased. In 1945, the majority of the surviving historic objects was destroyed, a fate shared by the port itself; all were rebuilt after the war. The particularly valuable crane on the Motława, a twin-towered Gothic gate from the mid-15th century with an inbuilt wooden port crane reconstructed after the war, accommodates the Central Maritime Museum. Shipbuilding represents an important branch of Gdańsk industry. The Gdańsk Shipyard constructs ocean liners as well as merchant and fishing vessels for the home market and foreign clients. On 16 December 1980, a Monument to the Fallen Shipyard Workers was unveiled in front of the shipyard gate to commemorate the tragic events of the 1970 strikes, and as a symbol of systemic transformations in Poland. The Independent Trade Union "Solidarity" was born in August 1980 in Gdańsk; in time, it expanded into a mass-scale social movement which in 1989 led to fundamental political changes, putting

on the left:

Gdańsk.

Sunset in the port.

an end to communist monopoly on state government. The port, extensively destroyed (55%) in the last war, was re-opened already in July 1945. During the inter-war period, it was the largest transshipment port on the Baltic littoral. In the 1970s, it was no longer large enough for the growing traffic of modern ships, thus necessitating the construction of the Northern Port, adapted to receive large ocean-going vessels and to render possible bulk-cargo transshipment, mainly coal and liquid fuels.

The first shots of the second world war were fired in Gdańsk at dawn on 1 September 1939. They came from the German battleship "Schleswig-Holstein", which had just arrived in the port on an official visit and started a cannonade aimed against the Polish base on Westerplatte peninsula, the site of the Polish Military Transport Depot. At the same time, the Germans attacked the Polish Post Office in Heweliusz Square in the Old Town. The 182 defenders of Westerplatte put up a heroic resistance for seven days. The German command deployed superior land, sea and air forces, which in the course of six days carried out sixteen unsuccessful attacks. The last assault, launched on 7 September, also failed, but the Poles, who had run out of ammunition and whose defence stands had been totally destroyed, were forced to surrender. In 1966, a monument was put up as a tribute to the Defenders of the Coast. (I. J. K.)

The history of local museums has been connected with the post-Franciscan monastery since 1848. The cross vaulted interiors are among the most beautiful in Gdańsk, and provide a harmonious background to the rich mediaeval collections, including the important. *Crucifixion* from Starogard and *St. George* from the Court of Arthur. The partly salvaged 19th-century collection amassed by Jakob Kabrun is composed of noteworthy paintings, drawings and illustrations, primarily from 17th-century Low Countries schools. Earlier art from The Netherlands is best represented by *The Last Judgment* riptych, a masterpiece attributed to Hans Memling.

The extremely rich crafts collections are composed predominantly of diverse exhibits from Gdańsk workshops, which from the 14th century were renowned in Poland for their gold artifacts, furniture, and metal and ceramic products. The Museum features liturgical vestments from the 14th-16th century, 17th- and 18th-century Gdańsk furniture, and a large collection of European faience, including rare Swedish examples. The gallery of Polish art displays works ranging from the 17th to the 20th century.

In the 18th century, Gdańsk was a major centre of ceramics production: beautiful tile stoves and faience vessels. The distinctive decoration consisted of pseudo-Chinese genre scenes and fantastic plants, paint-

ed on a white background. Goldsmithery flourished particularly during the 17th century, and Gdańsk artists were entrusted with all the important commissions in the Commonwealth. Coins and medallions were used to elaborately decorate vessels, often of imposing sizes. (P. T.)

Gdańsk and the neighbouring towns of Sopot and Gdynia constitute a single urban agglomeration known as the Tri-City. Sopot performs a role different than the one ascribed to the two larger cities: it is a popular seaside resort and spa, which evolved from a fishing village belonging to the Cistercians

from the 13th to the 18th century. Already in the mid-16th century it was the favourite summer resort of the Gdańsk townspeople. Having achieved urban status in 1901, Sopot grew into a fashionable and suitably outfitted resort. Affluent holidaymakers willingly visit the Grand Hotel, acclaimed for its excellent cuisine. The 512 metres-long pier is popular among strollers. Another local attraction is the only Forest Opera in Poland, situated among charming hills and the site of an annual international song competition.

Gdynia, another former Cistercian village (12th-18th century), is one of Poland's three main ports. In

Gdynia Orłowo. Fragment of the coastline.

1920, the Polish government decided to build a port having failed to secure favourable conditions in the port of Gdańsk. A ceremonial consecration of Gdynia as "a temporary military port and harbour for fishermen" took place in April 1923; the first ocean-going ship came in August. In 1926, Gdynia was granted urban status, and by 1939 it grew into a large town and one of Europe's most modern ports. At the time of its liberation (March 1945), the port was almost completely destroyed by the retreating Germans and its entrance was blocked by the sunken wreck of the

"Gneisenau". The port was reopened as early as April 1945. The town, port and shipyard were reconstructed and enlarged. Today, the port of Gdynia specialises primarily in general-cargo transshipment, and the shipyard builds vessels of the largest tonnage. (I.J.K.)

The Hel Peninsula, stretching from the northern part of the Kaszuby Littoral to the centre of the Bay of Gdańsk, is an attractive area for summer holidaymakers. The local resorts are located in former fishing settlements. The fishing village of Hel, at the far

Hel. Fishermen's
houses.

end of the peninsula, was founded probably in 1128 and contains a Gothic church (14th-15th century), converted into a Museum of Fishing, an 18th-century inn, and wooden, skeleton-construction fishermen's houses from the 19th century. A port was constructed here in the 19th century; during the interwar period, Hel prospered as a seaside resort. On 2 October 1939, it was one of the last outposts of Polish armed resistance to capitulate.

The resort of Jastarnia dates back to a 16th-century fishing settlement. The Hel Peninsula has been cre-ated by the wind and the sea, piling up sand dunes later overgrown by pine trees. Beaches stretch along both sides of the peninsula; the ones facing the sea are sandy, while those framing the bay are silty. (I. J. K.)

We owe two of the most valuable architectural monuments in Gdańsk Pomerania to the Cistercian monks: the monastery at Oliwa from 1188 and the one at Pelplin, founded in 1274. Today, both churches fulfil the function of cathedrals. The slender Late Baroque façade of Oliwa Cathedral, framed by two

Reformation onslaught. A large collection of paintings and sculptures represents predominantly assorted Mannerist and Rococo forms. The former main altar, executed by Wolfgang Sporer of Gdańsk in the northern arm of the transept, is a superb example of Mannerist sculpture from the early 17th century. Mannerism also prevails in the Kos family tombstone conceived by Willem van den Blocke of Flanders. The northern nave and the ambulatory contain more than a dozen Baroque altars made of marble. The Late Baroque fashioned the magnificent organ prospectus from 1763-1788. Compressed air mechanisms set into motion tens of angels, stars and the Sun. The Rococo abbey palace from 1754-1756 stands next to the cathedral amidst a Baroque garden, with a slightly later landscape park stretching beyond. (P. T.)

The cathedral in Pelplin, a town on the Wierzyca near Starogard Gdański, is a more uniform complex. Its Gothic form, built on the plan of a basilica with a well-defined transept, dates from the late 13th century. The desire to maintain a single architectural style is reflected in the Late Gothic nave vaulting from 1558. The long nave, endowed with exemplary proportions, is closed by a huge main altar (25 m high) from 1630, displaying *The Coronation of the Madonna* by Hermann Han, a reputed Mannerist painter whose best works were intended for Pelplin. Portraits by Bartholomew Strobel, court artist to Władysław IV, are accompanied by numerous compositions by Andrzej Stech, a talented eclectic artist of the Baroque era. Carved wooden stalls from the second half of the 15th century are among the most valuable examples of the crafts. The Diocesan Museum, arranged in the monastery, possesses notable art treasures. (P. T.)

The Kaszuby Lake District forms the most easterly and, at the same time, the highest part of the Pomeranian Lake District. The steep moraine hills are divided by deep river valleys or chutes filled with lakes as well as by marshes and peat bogs, the residues of former lakes. The river Radunia, flowing

Pelplin. Altar in the cathedral of the Assumption of the Holy Virgin Mary.

on the right:
Pelplin. Cathedral façade.

Gothic towers crowned with cupolas, was erected in several stages. The construction of the Late Romanesque building with a transept, partly preserved in the narrow southern nave, lasted to the middle of the 13th century. Following a fire in 1350, the church was significantly extended and elevated, the presbytery received an ambulatory, and a monastery was added on the south side. The interior was outfitted from the late 16th century to the end of the 18th century, and reflects the Counter-

**Bytów.
Teutonic Order
castle.**

1405, the Carthusians built a monastic complex and founded a settlement. Wars raging in the 15th and 17th century ruined the prospering monastery and settlement. During the first partition of Poland, the whole Kartuzy region was incorporated into Prussia, the Carthusian estates were confiscated (1772), and in 1826 the order was dissolved; the majority of the buildings belonging to the monastery was pulled down. Extant fragments of the complex, including the Gothic church with an unusual, coffin-shaped roof, redesigned in the second half of the 19th century, and the adjoining refectory and hermitage, can still be admired. Every July, Carthusian Organ Concerts are given in the church.

To the west, the Kaszuby Lake District adjoins the Bytów Lake District. Its main town is Bytów, now a small industrial and tourist centre, which evolved upon the basis of an ancient Slavonic stronghold (9th-10th century). The borough changed hands a number of times: to the 13th century, it belonged to the tribe of the Polanie, and from 1320 it was ruled for a century by the Teutonic Order. In 1455, Kazimierz Jagiellon granted the fief of Bytów to the dukes of West Pomerania; after the death of the last member of this dynastic line (1637) Bytów was annexed by Royal Prussia. Already in 1657, the Welawa-Bydgoszcz treaty signed during the reign of Jan Kazimierz handed Bytów over to the Elector of Brandenburg as a fief in return for assistance rendered to Poland during the war against the Swedes. In the Prussian partition area, Bytów acted as a major centre of opposition against Germanisation policies. In 1919, the Treaty of Versailles granted the borough to Germany despite the protests of the Polish inhabitants. In 1945, the devastated town (about 70% lay in ruins) returned to Poland and was rebuilt. Its foremost monuments include the mighty Gothic castle, built in 1399-1405, expanded by the dukes of Pomerania (16th-17th century) and redesigned in the 19th century. Today, it houses the Western Kaszuby Museum. (I. J. K.)

The landscape of the longest stretch of the Polish seacoast, known as the Słowiński Littoral, extending

in a deep gorge, cuts across the hills and carries water from the longest glacial chute in the region, which contains ten lakes. The biggest lake, named after the river, is Lake Raduńskie, 1 125 hectares large and up to 43 m deep, surrounded by farmland. Lake Ostrzyckie, further to the south and immediately at the foot of Mt. Wieżyca, the highest peak in the Lake District, is situated among charming beech forests. The region is popular among holidaymakers for its water sports and vacation facilities. The whole Kaszuby Lake District is part of a recreational infrastructure intended for the Tri-City agglomeration.

The town of Kartuzy, the main centre of a region famous for its folklore, derives its name from the Carthusian monks, brought over from Bohemia by Piotr of Rusocin, a Pomeranian magnate. In 1380-

westwards from the Kaszuby Littoral, is composed of salt tolerant plant life. The Słowinski Littoral offers excellent conditions for recreation; hence the numerous holiday and touris resorts. The old fishing settlement of Łeba, invitingly situated between the sea and two coastal lakes: Lake Łebskie and Lake Sarbskie, is the most important tourist centre in the eastern part of the Belt.

The Słowiński National Park, created to the west of Łeba, contains the largest complex of shifting sand dunes in Poland (up to 35m high), the lagoon lakes of Łebsko and Gardno, whose shaols comprise a strictly protected reservation with a great variety of water and a wading fowl, and Rowokół, the sacred hill of the Pomeranian tribes. The Park is also the site of villages formerly belonging to Słowinie, a Pomeranian ethnic group closely related to the Kaszub people. In this inaccessible terrain, the Słowinie protected themselves against Germanisation and managed to prserve their language, customs and traditional building style the longest. An ethnographic museum was opened in one of the farmsteads in the village of Kulki, where a number of typical cottages has survived. (I.J.K.)

The fishing settlement of Darłowo developed above the mouth of the River Wieprza alongside a Pomeranian tribal stronghold. It obtained municipal rights in 1312, and joined the Hanseatic League in 1361. Together with the whole of Western Pomerania Darłowo came under the rule of Brandenburg; subsequently, after the death of the last representative of the Piast dukes of Pomerania it was annexed by Prussia by virtue of the Peace of Westphalia (1648). The town, which returned to Poland in 1945, contains valuable historical monuments, largely from the period of the Pomeranian dukes, including the cemetery chapel of St. Gertrude from the first half of the 15th century, a characteristic example of Pomeranian architecture. The regional museum in the Castle of the Pomeranian Dukes features interesting collections of furniture, works of art and Pomeranian ethnography as well as Oriental art. Today, Darłowo is a fishing port and a local centre of fish processing.

The Drawsko Lake District occupies the southern part of the Koszalin voivodeship, one of the most beautiful fragments of the whole series of Polish lake districts. The largest lakes are Drawsko and Wielimie; linked by rivers, they create attractive canoe routes through varied terrain. The principal tourist centres are Szczecinek, Czaplinek and Połczyn Zdrój, the latter being also a well-known spa (sorrel, saline and therapeutic mud baths). The village of Stare Drawsko, situated on an isthmus between the Drawsko and Żerdno lakes, was the site of Drahim Castle built in the second half of the 14th century and belonging to the Joannites. An 18th-century fire left behind ruins, today visited by sightseers. (I. J. K.)

Darłowo.
Fishing boat.

on pages 334-335:

Słowiński National Park. Shifting sand dunes.

Henryk of Braniewo, one of the most celebrated architects in the second half of the 14th century, was capable of rejecting Gothic schemes and offering new architectural solutions, which involved the integration of interiors by liquidating the unconnected presbytery. He also attached considerable attention to exterior decoration, and applied the delicate and lacey patterns produced by colourful, glazed ceramic bricks. Henryk was the author of the church of St. James in Szczecin, but his foremost work was the expanded church of the Holy Virgin Mary in Stargard Szczeciński. This brick hall construction from the end of the 13th century was adapted into an enormous basilica with an ambulatory and the Holy Virgin Mary chapel on the axis. In the 17th century, the impressive, spacious interior of the church was given Neo-Gothic vaulting. The nearby town hall, completed in 1569, has retained its Late Gothic forms, discernible especially in the gable. (P. T.)

The seaside resort and fishing, passenger and sailing port of Kamień Pomorski is situated on the River Dziwna on the Szczecin Littoral, in the western part of the Polish coastline. In the 9th-10th century, Kamień was a port and castle-town of the Wolinianie tribe; later, it became the capital of Western Pomerania, and from 1175 – the seat of a bishopric. Municipal status was granted in 1274, and from the 14th

Stargard Szczeciński. Town hall.

on the left:

Stargard Szczeciński. Town houses, in the background – the church of the Holy Virgin Mary.

Kamień Pomorski.
Cathedral, organs.

century the borough belonged to the Hanseatic League. In 1630, Kamień was seized by the Swedes, but already in 1679 it was captured by Brandenburg. The beginnings of a seaside resort are connected with the discovery of saline springs in 1876. In 1945, the town was the object of fierce battles; liberated by Polish forces, the gravely devastated Kamień (about 65% lay in ruins) was rebuilt. Similarly to all the towns on the Szczecin Littoral, Kamień has many valuable historic monuments: a preserved mediaeval urban layout, fragments of the 13th-- and 14th-century town walls, including the Wolin Gate, a Late Gothic town hall from the 15th century, a bishop's palace (14th-15th century), an 18th-century canons' manor house, and town houses from the 18th and 19th century. The most highly prized architectural relic is the town cathedral: a Late Romanesque-Early Gothic basilica with a

on the left:

Kamień Pomorski.
Cathedral, cloister
garden, 14th century.

Trzęsacz.
Ruins of a church.

on the right:
Szczecin. Castle of
the dukes of
Pomerania.

transept (12th-13th century) containing a beautiful Baroque organ from the 17th century. The cathedral treasury protects collections of archaeological findings, sacral art works and old prints. (I. J. K.)

The Szczecin Estuary, the river mouth of the Odra, is the remnant of a much more extensive sea bay. Today, it has an area of 968 sq. km, of which about a half belongs to Poland. The shallow bay (4-7 m) is linked with the sea by three straits created by the Piana, Świna and Dziwna rivers. The islands of Wolin and Uznam separate the bay from the Baltic Sea. The salinity of the water is slight due to the hampered flow of sea water via the straits, and the large

influx of river water. The Szczecin Estuary is an important shipping route, but requires constant regulation of depth and dredging the water lane. It is also an important fishing area, where fresh-water and sea-water species abound (roach, bream, pike perch, pike, eel and perch). (I. J . K.)

On the high left bank of the Odra, not far from the river's estuary, lies Szczecin, a large sea port and an important industrial, cultural and academic centre. Originally, Szczecin was an ancient Slav settlement from the Lusatian culture period (Early Bronze Age). In the 9th century, a large stronghold was built on Castle Hill, with a crafts-trading settlement below. In

967, Mieszko I incorporated Szczecin and the whole of Pomerania into Poland, but after the death of Bolesław the Brave (1025) the borough regained its independence as a merchants' republic. In 1121, it was conquered by Bolesław the Wrymouth, and in 1237 – it received municipal status. As a member of the Hanseatic League Szczecin became the foremost trading centre in Western Pomerania (13th-14th century). At the end of the 15th century, Duke Bogusław X transferred the ducal capital of Western Pomerania here, and built a large castle. The Thirty Years' War brought great losses to the town, which in 1630 was occupied by the Swedes. In the aftermath of the Northern War Szczecin passed into Prussian hands (1713), and became strongly fortified (1840). Sea trade was revived and manufacturing developed under the Prussians. At the turn of the 19th century, industry and port facilities were expanded and a new city centre developed on the site of the Prussian fortifications. Szczecin attracted numerous Poles from Greater Poland and Pomerania, many of whom emigrated to the reborn Polish state after 1918. The political and economic situation altered by the Versailles Treaty led to the port's decline in favour of Hamburg and Gdynia. Many factories closed down due to the great economic crisis of 1929-1933. The immense losses suffered during the second world war totalled about 65% of all buildings and nearly 95% of the local industry and port facilities. Almost immediately after Szczecin was taken over by the Polish authorities the port, industrial enterprises and town were rebuilt and then enlarged. The restoration of the city's hinterland greatly contributed to postwar revival, and Szczecin became an important transshipment and transit port for Czech, Hungarian and German cargo. Its industries have been expanded together with the cultural and academic functions of the town. The characteristic stellar urban layout of the radiating City streets and squares was replicated, and new public buildings and housing estates were completed. The Chrobry Embankment, with its early 20th-century monumental edifices, regained its stately nature. Many of Szczecin's important historic buildings have been rebuilt or partially recon-

structed, including the St. James Cathedral, a Gothic hall church, and the castle of the dukes of Pomerania, whose façade, typical for a Renaissance residence from the second half of the 16th century and the beginning of the 17th century, was restored.
(I. J. K.)

The collections of the National Museum in Szczecin, whose most valuable exhibits are mediaeval works of art, developed in the 19th century thanks to a campaign intent on protecting monuments deteriorating in local mediaeval churches. In 1928, the collection was installed in a palace from 1727. The mediaeval and modern art department features outstanding examples of sculpted wooden and stone objects from the 13th-16th century, including an interesting complex of Romanesque-Gothic sculptures from Gotland. Renaissance art is associated primarily with the patronage of the dukes of Western Pomerania. The crafts collection is equally rich. A gallery of 19th-- and 20th-century Polish art was opened in 1948. An African ethnographic collection has been recently expanded thanks to research conducted by the Museum in Mali. The majority of the featured works is closely linked with Western Pomerania. *The Crucified* from Kamień Pomorski Cathedral could be the work of Herman Walter of Kołobrzeg. This expressive

Pęzino.
Castle, 16th century.

on the left:
Szczecin.
Town houses in
market square.

mediaeval sculpture, one of the most beautiful of its sort, intentionally operates with deformation and contrast, while the execution of the head of Christ emphasises lyricism. The artist was well acquainted with English and Rhenish sculpture of the period, but produced an original work stemming from mediaeval mysticism. *The Madonna of Gardno*, associated with the patronage of the Cistercian monastery at Kołbacz, has been linked with sculpture from Gotland, and is an example of a transitory period when Romanesque forms mingled with the first symptoms of the new, Gothic approach. The bronze bolt from the door of the Kołobrzeg collegiate church has been cast in the shape of a lion's head surrounded by eight medallions entwined with a symbolic grapevine. The decorations on the medallions include symbols of the Evangelists. Presumably the work of Johan Apengeter, the bolt is a magnificent example of Gothic craftsmanship. (P. T.)

The islands of Wolin and Uznam, which close the Bay of Szczecin, are separated by the strait of the Świna. Wolin belongs to Poland, and Uznam is crossed by the border with Germany. In the 7th-9th century, this was the territory of the Wolinianie tribe, whose main settlement in the 9th century was the stronghold of Wolin. The artisan-trading settlement that developed near the stronghold was known as Julin, Jumne or Jomsborg, the centre of an independent merchants' republic. In 966, the traveller Ibrahim ibn Yaqub described Wolin as the most powerful borough on the Baltic coast. At the end of the 11th century, Wolin started to lose its rank in favour of Szczecin. Conquered by the dukes of Pomerania and Christianised, in 1140 it became the seat of a bishopric. The competition of Szczecin and Kamień Pomorski as well as the silting over of the Dźwina led to a gradual decline of Wolin, culminated by the Danish invasions of 1170-1184 and the transference of the bishopric to Kamień Pomorski. The *locatio* of the town in 1178, performed according to German law, did not restore its former position. Today, Wolin is a

minor market centre with small-scale food and timber industries, known above all as a popular seaside resort thanks to its interesting past and picturesque location. An additional attraction is the Wolin National Park, established in 1960, which encompasses the central part of Wolin Island – a moraine high land with lakes and cliffs overhanging the Baltic and the Bay of Szczecin. A large part of the Park is overgrown with beech woods; strict reservations protect unique species of the local flora, such as the Pomeranian beechwood with wild orchids in the undergrowth, or the Pomeranian woodbine. The park is inhabited by numerous species of water fowl, and the Bay of Pomerania is a natural habitat of the grey seal and the porpoise.

Międzyzdroje, one of the largest and best known resorts on the Polish seacoast and a spa (saline and mud baths), lies at the western end of the Wolin National Park. From 1997, a summer film festival held here gathers the fans and stars of the Polish cinema. The islands at the mouth of the Świna along the western end of the Polish coastline form a town known as Świnoujście, whose centre is located on the island of Uznam. Although already in the 9th-10th century this was the site of a tribal stronghold of the Wolinianie and a ford used by traders, the actual development of Swinoujście was connected with the construction of a port in the 18th century. In the 19th century, Świnoujście became a seaside resort and a spa. Destroyed in 1945, it was rebuilt and expanded. Today, Świnoujście is a deep-water port receiving large vessels which cannot gain access to Szczecin because of the bay's shallowness. It is also the largest deep-sea fishing port in Poland, and a fish processing centre. The functions of a health and tourist resort have been retained. There are ferry services to Sweden and Denmark and hydrofoil boats to Szczecin; seagoing yachts set off for their frequently distant voyages. (I. J. K.)

INDEX

Poland: sites mentioned on the UNESCO list of world cultural and natural heritage

1978 ■ Historical City of Cracow
1978 ■ Salt mine in Wieliczka
1979 ■ The Auschwitz-Birkenau concentration camp terrains
1979 ■ The Białowieża National Park
1980 ■ Old Town in Warsaw
1992 ■ Old Town in Zamość
1997 ■ Old Town complex in Toruń
1997 ■ The Teutonic Order castle in Malbork
1999 ■ Kalwaria Zebrzydowska: architectural-landscape complex
2001 ■ Peace churches in Jawor and Swidnica
2003 ■ Wooden churches in Binarowa, Dębno, Lipnica Murowana, Sękowa, Haczów and Blizne
2004 ■ Park Mużakowski / Muskaner Park
2006 ■ Centennial Hall in Wrocław

© by Wydawnictwo „Arkady" Sp. z o.o., Warszawa 2004, 2005, 2007, 2010
All rights reserved
Graphic design: Katarzyna Aderek
Translation: Aleksandra Chojnowska-Rodzińska
Index: Krystyna Śliwa
Editing: Ewa Cander
Proofreading: Danuta Brzezińska

ISBN 978-83-213-4275-9

On the book cover: Panoramic view of the Tatra mts.

All photographs by Mirosław and Maciej Ciunowiczowie,
with the exception of photographs on page:
13 (Krzysztof Plebankiewicz);
14-15 (Editor's Photo Archive);
105 top (Zofia Raczkowska);
170 (Teresa Żółtowska);
256-257 (Zofia Raczkowska);
268 (Zofia Raczkowska).

Wydawnictwo Arkady
00-344 Warszawa, ul. Dobra 28
tel. (022) 635 83 44
fax (022) 827 41 94
e-mail: info@arkady.com.pl
www.arkady-info.eu
Mail order bookstore, tel. (022) 826-70-79
Publisher bookstore, tel. (022) 828-40-20
Editing I (reprint), 2010. Index 3562/R
Illustration: 69 – Studio Reklamy, Olsztyn
Print: Olsztyńskie Zakłady Graficzne SA